100 words

ALMOST EVERYONE *confuses* AND *misuses*

HOUGHTON MIFFLIN HARCOURT
Boston New York

EDITORIAL AND PRODUCTION STAFF OF THE
American Heritage® Dictionaries

The staff wishes to acknowledge former Executive Editor Joseph Pickett along with Nicholas A. Durlacher, Uchenna C. Ikonné, Katherine M. Isaacs, Susan I. Spitz, and Patrick Taylor for their contributions in the 2004 edition of this title.

Visit our websites: hmhco.com *and* ahdictionary.com

LIBRARY OF CONGRESS CATALOGING-IN-PUBLICATION DATA
Names: Houghton Mifflin Harcourt Publishing Company.
Title: 100 words almost everyone confuses and misuses / The 100 Words series® From the Editors of the American Heritage® Dictionaries.
Other titles: One hundred words almost everyone confuses and misuses
Description: Boston : Houghton Mifflin Harcourt, [2016] | Series: "100 Words" series | Reissue of the third book in the "100 Words" series.
Identifiers: LCCN 2016005721 | ISBN 9780544791190 (paperback)
Subjects: LCSH: English language--Usage. | English language--Homonyms. | English language--Synonyms and antonyms. | BISAC: REFERENCE / Directories. | REFERENCE / Word Lists.
Classification: LCC PE1460 .A15 2016 | DDC 428.1--dc23 LC record available at https://lccn.loc.gov/2016005721

Text design by Anne Chalmers

MANUFACTURED IN THE UNITED STATES OF AMERICA

1 2 3 4 5 6 7 8 9 10 - DOC - 21 20 19 18 17 16

4500606363

Preface

The editors of the *American Heritage* dictionaries are pleased to reissue the third book in our "100 Words" series, *100 Words Almost Everyone Confuses and Misuses,* 12 years after its initial publication. This has long been one of the best sellers in this popular series, which has grown to include 14 titles. Language usage shifts and changes over time, and every year we ballot our Usage Panel (see ahdictionary.com/word/usagepanel.html for more information and the current list of Panelists) to analyze the most recent trends in language usage. This updated edition incorporates results from our latest ballots to reflect the current status of problematic usages.

This book is for people who remember that their English teachers had something to say about how these words are used, but often forget what exactly was said. How do *flaunt* and *flout* differ? Why do people mispronounce *nuclear*? Is *kudos* singular or plural? This book gives you the answers! You'll learn how things can go wrong, and you'll learn how to make them right.

Entries, based on the content of the *American Heritage* dictionaries, are presented in an expanded layout that's easy to read and comprehend. Each word, such as *presently*, or each word group, such as *affect/effect*, is discussed in a note derived from the usage program of the *American Heritage* dictionaries. Additionally, we show the use of many words in context using quotations from a wide mix of classical novelists (Jane Austen, *Pride and Prejudice*; Mark Twain, *The Adventures of Tom Sawyer*), contemporary authors (Sebastian Junger, *The Perfect Storm*; William Least Heat-Moon, *River-Horse*) and current journalists (Jane E. Brody, *New York Times*; Chet Raymo, *Boston Globe*; Corby Kummer, *Atlantic Monthly*).

We hope that you will find *100 Words Almost Everyone Confuses and Misuses* to be a helpful reference book for improving your confidence in speaking and writing.

Steve Kleinedler,
Executive Editor

Guide to the Entries

ENTRY WORD The 100 words that constitute this book are listed alphabetically. The entry words, along with inflected and derived forms, are divided into syllables by centered dots. These dots show you where you would break the word at the end of a line. The pronunciation of the word follows the entry word. Please see the key on page vii for an explanation of the pronunciation system.

PART OF SPEECH At least one part of speech follows each entry word. The part of speech tells you the grammatical category that the word belongs to. Parts of speech include *noun, adjective, adverb, transitive verb,* and *intransitive verb.* (A transitive verb is a verb that needs an object to complete its meaning. *Wash* is a transitive verb in the sentence *I washed the car.* The direct object of *wash* is *the car.* An intransitive verb is one that does not take an object, as *sleep* in the sentence *I slept for seven hours.* Many verbs are both transitive and intransitive.)

INFLECTIONS A word's inflected forms differ from the main entry form by the addition of a suffix or by a change in the base form to indicate grammatical features such as number, person, or tense. They are set in boldface type, divided into syllables, and given pronunciations as necessary. The past tense, past participle, and the third person singular present tense inflections of all verbs are shown. The plurals of nouns are shown when they are spelled in a way other than by adding *s* to the base form.

LABELS The USAGE PROBLEM label warns of possible difficulties involving grammar, diction, or writing style. A word or definition with this label is discussed in a Usage Note, as at **flaunt**.

ORDER OF SENSES Entries having more than one sense are arranged with the central and often the most commonly sought meanings first. In an entry with more than one part of speech, the senses are numbered in separate sequences after each part of speech, as at **average**.

EXAMPLES OF USAGE Examples often follow the definitions and are set in italic type. These examples show the entry words in typical contexts. Sometimes the examples are quotations from authors of books. These quotations are shown within quotation marks, and the quotation's author and source are shown.

ETYMOLOGIES Etymologies appear in square brackets following the last definition. An etymology traces the history of a word as far back in time as can be determined with reasonable certainty. The stage most closely preceding Modern English is given first, with each earlier stage following in sequence. A language name, linguistic form (in italics), and brief definition of the form are given for each stage of the derivation. To avoid redundancy, a language, form, or definition is not repeated if it is identical to the corresponding item in the immediately preceding stage. Occasionally, a form will be given that is not actually preserved in written documents but which scholars are confident did exist—such a form will be marked by an asterisk (*). The word *from* is used to indicate origin of any kind: by inheritance, borrowing, or derivation. When an etymology splits a compound word into parts, a colon introduces the parts and each element is then traced back to its origin, with those elements enclosed in parentheses.

RELATED WORDS At the end of many entries, additional boldface words appear without definitions. These words are related in basic meaning to the entry word and are usually formed from the entry word by the addition of suffixes.

NOTES Some entries include Usage Notes that present important information and guidance on matters of grammar, diction, pronunciation, and nuances. Some refer to responses from our Usage Panel, a group of over 200 respected writers, scholars, and critics. The editors of the *American Heritage* dictionaries regularly survey these people on a broad range of usage questions.

Pronunciation Guide

Pronunciations appear in parentheses after boldface entry words. If a word has more than one pronunciation, the first pronunciation is usually more common than the other, but often they are equally common. Pronunciations are shown after inflections and related words where necessary.

Stress is the relative degree of emphasis that a word's syllables are spoken with. An unmarked syllable has the weakest stress in the word. The strongest, or primary, stress is indicated with a bold mark (**ʹ**). A lighter mark (ʹ) indicates a secondary level of stress. The stress mark follows the syllable it applies to. Words of one syllable have no stress mark because there is no other stress level that the syllable can be compared to.

The key on page vii shows the pronunciation symbols used in this book. To the right of the symbols are words that show how the symbols are pronounced. The letters whose sound corresponds to the symbols are shown in boldface.

The symbol (ə) is called *schwa.* It represents a vowel with the weakest level of stress in a word. The schwa sound varies slightly according to the vowel it represents or the sounds around it:

a·bun·dant (ə-bŭn**ʹ**dənt)
mo·ment (mō**ʹ**mənt)
civ·il (sĭv**ʹ**əl)
grate·ful (grāt**ʹ**fəl)

PRONUNCIATION KEY			
Symbol	**Examples**	**Symbol**	**Examples**
ă	**pat**	oi	n**oi**se
ā	**pay**	o͝o	t**oo**k
âr	**care**	o͝or	l**ure**
ä	f**a**ther	o͞o	b**oo**t
b	**bib**	ou	**ou**t
ch	**church**	p	**pop**
d	**deed**, mill**ed**	r	**roar**
ĕ	**pet**	s	**sauce**
ē	**bee**	sh	**ship**, **dish**
f	**fife**, **ph**ase, rou**gh**	t	**tight**, stopp**ed**
g	**gag**	th	**th**in
h	**h**at	*th*	**th**is
hw	**wh**ich	ŭ	**cut**
ĭ	**pit**	ûr	**ur**ge, **ter**m, **fir**m, **wor**d, **hear**d
ī	**pie**, **b**y	v	**valve**
îr	**deer**, **pier**	w	**w**ith
j	**judge**	y	**y**es
k	**kick**, **c**at, pi**que**	z	**z**ebra, **x**ylem
l	**l**id, need**le**	zh	vi**s**ion, plea**s**ure, gara**ge**
m	**mum**		
n	**n**o, sudd**en**		
ng	thi**ng**		
ŏ	**pot**	ə	**a**bout, it**e**m, ed**i**ble, gall**o**p, circ**u**s
ō	**toe**		
ô	**caught**, **paw**		
ôr	**core**	ər	butt**er**

"Then a dog began to howl somewhere in a farmhouse far down the road—a long, agonized wailing, as if from fear. . . . Then, far off in the distance, from the mountains on each side of us began a louder and a sharper howling—that of wolves—which **affected** both the horses and myself in the same way—for I was minded to jump from the caleche and run, whilst they reared again and plunged madly, so that the driver had to use all his great strength to keep them from bolting."

—Bram Stoker,
Dracula

1

ad·verse (ăd-vûrs′, ăd′vûrs′)

adjective

1. Acting or serving to oppose; antagonistic: *"And let thy blows, doubly redoubled, / Fall like amazing thunder on the casque / Of thy adverse pernicious enemy"* (William Shakespeare, *King Richard II*). **2.** Contrary to one's interests or welfare; harmful or unfavorable: *"[M]ost companies are fearful of adverse publicity and never report internal security breaches . . . to law enforcement agencies, security analysts contend"* (Peter H. Lewis, *New York Times*). **3.** Moving in an opposite direction: *As it ascended, the balloon was caught in an adverse current and drifted out to sea.*

[Middle English, from Old French *advers,* from Latin *adversus,* past participle of *advertere,* to turn toward : *ad-*, ad- + *vertere,* to turn.]

RELATED WORD:

adverb—**ad·verse′ly**

SEE NOTE AT **averse** (# 13).

2

af·fect[1] (ə-fĕkt′)

transitive verb

Past participle and past tense: **af·fect·ed**
Present participle: **af·fect·ing**
Third person singular present tense: **af·fects**

1. To have an influence on or effect a change in: *Inflation affects the buying power of the dollar.* **2.** To act on the emotions of; touch or move: "*Then, far off in the distance, from the mountains on each side of us began a louder and a sharper howling—that of wolves—which affected both the horses and myself in the same way*" (Bram Stoker, *Dracula*). **3.** To attack or infect, as a disease: *Rheumatic fever is one of many afflictions that can affect the heart.*

noun (ăf′ĕkt′)

1. Feeling or emotion, especially as manifested by facial expression or body language: "*The soldiers seen on television had been carefully chosen for blandness of affect*" (Norman Mailer, *Vanity Fair*). **2.** *Obsolete* A disposition, feeling, or tendency.

[Middle English *affecten,* from Latin *afficere, affect-,* to do to, act on : *ad-,* ad- + *facere,* to do.]

SEE NOTE AT **effect** (# 28).

3

af·fect[2] (ə-fĕkt′)

transitive verb

Past participle and past tense: **af·fect·ed**
Present participle: **af·fect·ing**
Third person singular present tense: **af·fects**

1. To put on a false show of; simulate: *"He wheedled, bribed, ridiculed, threatened, and scolded; affected indifference, that he might surprise the truth from her"* (Louisa May Alcott, *Little Women*). **2.** To have or show a liking for: *affects dramatic clothes.* **3.** To tend to by nature; tend to assume: *In my chemistry class, we study substances that affect crystalline form.* **4.** To imitate; copy: *"Spenser, in affecting the ancients, writ no language"* (Ben Jonson, *Timber*).

[Middle English *affecten,* from Latin *affectāre,* to strive after, frequentative of *afficere, affect-,* to affect, influence; see AFFECT[1].]

RELATED WORD:

noun—**af·fect′er**

SEE NOTE AT **effect** (# 28).

ag·gra·vate (ăg′rə-vāt′)

transitive verb

Past participle and past tense: **ag·gra·vat·ed**
Present participle: **ag·gra·vat·ing**
Third person singular present tense: **ag·gra·vates**

1. To make worse or more troublesome: *"Drinking alcohol (especially heavy drinking) or taking tranquilizers or sedating antihistamines shortly before bedtime can aggravate snoring by reducing muscle tone"* (Jane E. Brody, *New York Times*). **2.** To rouse to exasperation or anger; provoke.

[Latin *aggravāre, aggravāt-* : *ad-*, ad- + *gravāre,* to burden (from *gravis,* heavy).]

RELATED WORDS:

adverb—**ag′gra·vat′ing·ly**
adjective—**ag′gra·va′tive**
noun—**ag′gra·va′tor**

Aggravate comes from the Latin verb *aggravāre,* which meant "to make heavier," that is, "to add to the weight of." It also had the extended senses "to burden" or "to oppress." On the basis of this etymology, some claim that *aggravate* should not be used to mean "to irritate, annoy, rouse to anger." But such senses for the word date back to the 17th century and are pervasive. In our 2005 survey, 83 percent of the Usage Panel accepted this usage in the sentence *It's the endless wait for luggage that aggravates me the most about air travel.* This was a significant increase from the 68 percent who accepted the same sentence in 1988.

5

al·leged (ə-lĕjd′, ə-lĕj′ĭd)

adjective

Represented as existing or as being as described but not so proved; supposed: *"Cryptozoology is the study of unexplained and alleged sightings of strange creatures not documented by standard zoology"* (Chet Raymo, *Boston Globe*).

RELATED WORD:

adverb—**al·leg′ed·ly**

An *alleged* burglar is someone who has been accused of being a burglar but against whom no charges have been proved. An *alleged* incident is an event that is said to have taken place but has not yet been verified. In their zeal to protect the rights of the accused, newspapers and law enforcement officials sometimes misuse *alleged.* Someone arrested for murder may be only an *alleged* murderer, for example, but is a real, not an *alleged,* suspect in that his or her status as a suspect is not in doubt. Similarly, if the money from a safe is known to have been stolen and not merely mislaid, then we may safely speak of a theft without having to qualify our description with *alleged.*

6

all right (ôl rīt)

adjective

1. In good condition or working order; satisfactory: *The mechanic checked to see if the tires were all right.* **2.** Acceptable; agreeable: *"Men are all right for friends, but as soon as you marry them they turn into cranky old fathers, even the wild ones"* (Willa Cather, *My Ántonia*). **3.** Average; mediocre: *The performance was just all right, not remarkable.* **4.** Correct: *These figures are perfectly all right.* **5.** Uninjured; safe: *The passengers were shaken up but are all right.*

adverb

1. In a satisfactory way; adequately: *"Cobol was designed to be somewhat readable by nonprogrammers. The idea was that managers could read through a printed listing of Cobol code to determine if the programmer got it all right. This has rarely happened"* (Charles Petzold, *New York Times*). **2.** Very well; yes. Used as a reply to a question or to introduce a declaration: *All right, I'll go.* **3.** Without a doubt: *"They* [Bonobos] *are chimpanzees, all right, but almost the reverse of their more familiar cousins* (Phoebe-Lou Adams, *Atlantic Monthly*).

❧ Despite the frequent use of the form *alright* the single word spelling is still widely viewed as nonstandard. In our 2009 survey, more than two-thirds of the Usage Panel rejected *alright* in examples like *Don't worry. Everything will be alright,* whereas over 90 percent accepted *all right* in the same examples. This resistance may seem peculiar, since similar fusions incorporating *all,* such as *already* and *altogether,* have never raised any objections. The difference may lie in the fact that *already* and *altogether* became single words back in the Middle Ages, whereas *alright* has only been around for a little more than a century and was called out by language critics as a misspelling. Readers may view the use of *alright,* especially in formal writing, as an error or a willful breaking of convention.

7

al·to·geth·er (ôl′tə-gĕth′ər)

adverb

1. Entirely; completely; utterly: *The three-year-old, then, is a grammatical genius—master of most constructions . . . avoiding many kinds of errors altogether"* (Steven Pinker, *The Language Instinct).* **2.** With all included or counted; all told: *"There were altogether eight official Crusades"* (*The Reader's Companion to Military History,* Robert Cowley). **3.** On the whole; with everything considered: *Altogether, I'm sorry it happened.*

noun

A state of nudity. Often used with *the*: *The artist's model posed in the altogether.*

[Middle English *al togeder.*]

Altogether and *all together* do not mean the same thing. *Altogether* is an adverb that indicates totality or entirety: *I rarely eat tomatoes, and I avoid peppers altogether. All together* is an adverb that indicates that the members of a group perform or undergo an action collectively: *The nations stood all together. The prisoners were herded all together. All together* is used only in sentences that can be rephrased so that *all* and *together* may be separated by other words: *The books lay all together in a heap. All the books lay together in a heap.*

“The three-year-old, then, is a grammatical genius—master of most constructions, obeying rules far more often than flouting them, respecting language universals, erring in sensible, adultlike ways, and avoiding many kinds of errors **altogether**.”

—Steven Pinker,
The Language Instinct

8

a·mong (ə-mŭng′) also **a·mongst** (ə-mŭngst′)

preposition

1. In the midst of; surrounded by: *A tall oak tree grew among the pines.* **2.** In the group, number, or class of: *"Santería has a growing following among middle-class professionals, including white, black and Asian Americans"* (Lizette Alvarez, *New York Times*). **3.** In the company of; in association with: *I spent the summer in Europe traveling among a group of tourists.* **4.** By many or the entire number of; with many: *"It has long been a tradition among novel writers that a book must end by everybody getting just what they wanted, or if the conventional happy ending was impossible, then it must be a tragedy in which one or both should die"* (Molly Gloss, *Wild Life*). **5.** With portions to each of: *Distribute this among you.* **6.** With one another: *Don't fight among yourselves.*

[Middle English, from Old English *āmang* : *ā*, in + *gemang,* throng.]

SEE NOTE AT **between** (# 14).

9 **as·sure** (ə-sho͝or′)

transitive verb

Past participle and past tense: **as·sured**
Present participle: **as·sur·ing**
Third person singular present tense: **as·sures**

1. To inform positively, as to remove doubt: *The ticket agent assured us that the train would be on time.* **2.** To cause to feel sure: *The candidate assured the electorate that he would keep his promises.* **3.** To give confidence to; reassure: *"Katharine assured her by nodding her head several times, but the manner in which she left the room was not calculated to inspire complete confidence in her diplomacy"* (Virginia Woolf, *Night and Day*). **4.** To make certain; ensure: *"Let every nation know, whether it wishes us well or ill, that we shall pay any price, bear any burden, meet any hardship, support any friend, oppose any foe, in order to assure the survival and the success of liberty"* (John F. Kennedy, Inaugural Address). **5.** *Chiefly British* To insure, as against loss.

[Middle English *assuren,* from Old French *assurer,* from Vulgar Latin **assēcurāre,* to make sure : Latin *ad-*, ad- + Latin *sēcurus,* secure.]

RELATED WORDS:

adjective—**as·sur′a·ble**
noun—**as·sur′er, as·sur′or**

SEE NOTE AT **insure** (# 49).

10

au·ger (ô′gər)

noun

1a. Any of various hand tools, typically having a threaded shank and cross handle, used for boring holes in wood or ice: "[He] *can himself build a cabin with the three necessary implements: an ax, a broadax, and an auger*" (Michael Ennis, *Architectural Digest*). **b.** A drill bit. **2a.** A machine having a rotating helical shaft for boring into the earth. **b.** A rotating helical shaft used to convey material, as in a snow blower.

[Middle English, from *an auger,* alteration of *a nauger,* from Old English *nafogār,* auger.]

transitive verb

Past participle and past tense: **au·gered**
Present participle: **au·ger·ing**
Third person singular present tense: **au·gers**

To bore by means of an auger: *The fishermen augered a hole in the ice.*

SEE NOTE AT **augur** (# 11).

au·gur (ô′gər)

noun

1. One of a group of ancient Roman religious officials who foretold events by observing and interpreting signs and omens. **2.** A seer or prophet; a soothsayer.

verb

Past participle and past tense: **au·gured**
Present participle: **au·gur·ing**
Third person singular present tense: **au·gurs**

transitive **1.** To predict, especially from signs or omens; foretell. **2.** To serve as an omen of; betoken: *Early returns augured victory for the young candidate.*

intransitive **1.** To make predictions from signs or omens. **2.** To be a sign or omen: *A smooth dress rehearsal augured well for the play.*

[Middle English, from Latin.]

RELATED WORD:

adjective—**au′gu·ral** (ô′gyə-rəl)

☙ An *auger* is a tool used for boring holes. An *augur* is a seer or soothsayer. The verb *augur* means "to foretell or betoken," as in *A good, well-grounded education augurs success. Augur* is also commonly used in phrases such as *augur well* or *augur ill*, as in *The quarterback's injury augurs ill for the game.*

av·er·age (ăv′ər-ĭj, ăv′rĭj)

noun

1. The value obtained by dividing the sum of a set of quantities by the number of quantities in the set. Also called *arithmetic mean*: *The average of 2, 5, 8, and 11 is 6.5.* **2.** A number that is derived from and considered typical or representative of a set of numbers. **3.** A typical kind or usual level or degree: *"My basic athletic skills—quickness, speed, coordination, all those things—were a little above average, but what I could do better than anybody my age was anticipate what a pitcher was going to throw and where he was going to throw it"* (David Huddle, *The Story of a Million Years*). **4.** The ratio of a team's or player's successful performances such as wins, hits, or goals, divided by total opportunities for successful performance, such as games, times at bat, or shots: *The team finished the season with a .500 average.*

adjective

1. Computed or determined as an average: *"By ten o'clock average windspeed is forty knots out of the north-northeast, spiking to twice that and generating a huge sea"* (Sebastian Junger, *The Perfect Storm*). **2.** Being intermediate between extremes, as on a scale: *The teacher offered extra help for students with average grades.* **3.** Usual or ordinary in kind or character: *The firm conducted a poll of average people.*

verb

Past participle and past tense: **av·er·aged**

Present participle: **av·er·ag·ing**

Third person singular present tense: **av·er·ag·es**

transitive **1.** To calculate the average of: *The teacher explained how to average a set of numbers.* **2.** To do or have an average of: *The part-time employee averaged three hours of work a day.*

intransitive To be or amount to an average: *Our expenses averaged out to 45 dollars per day.*

[From Middle English *averay,* charge above the cost of freight, from Old French *avarie,* from Old Italian *avaria,* duty, from Arabic *'awārīya,* damaged goods, from *'awār,* blemish, from *'awira,* to be damaged.]

RELATED WORD:

noun—**av′er·age·ness**

SEE NOTE AT **median** (# 63).

13

a·verse (ə-vûrs′)

adjective

Having a feeling of opposition, distaste, or aversion; strongly disinclined: *"Cheating on schoolwork has simmered on as long as there have been students averse to studying"* (Christina McCarroll, *Christian Science Monitor*).

[Latin *āversus*, past participle of *āvertere*, to turn away.]

RELATED WORDS:

adverb—**a·verse′ly**
noun—**a·verse′ness**

Who isn't *averse* to getting *adverse* reactions to their ideas? *Averse* normally refers to people and means "having a feeling of distaste or aversion," as in *As an investor I'm averse to risk-taking.* People sometimes mistakenly slip in *adverse* for *averse* in these constructions with *to*. However, *adverse* normally does not refer to people, but rather to things that are antagonistic or contrary to someone's interests. Thus we say *We're working under very adverse* (not *averse) circumstances* and *All the adverse* (not *averse) criticism frayed the new mayor's nerves.*

14

be·tween (bĭ-twēn′)

preposition

1a. In or through the position or interval separating: *"The shapes of the shoulder bones indicate that the animal may have swung by its arms between the branches of trees"* (Lisa Guernsey, *Chronicle of Higher Education*); *"Between 1970 and 1995, the average American's yearly sugar consumption increased from 120 pounds to 150 pounds"* (Richard A. Knox, *Boston Globe*). **b.** Intermediate to, as in quantity, amount, or degree: *It costs between 15 and 20 dollars.* **2.** Connecting over or through a space that is separating: *I walked down the long path between the cabin and the lake.* **3.** USAGE PROBLEM Associating or uniting in a reciprocal action or relationship: *The mediator hammered out an agreement between workers and management. The professor noted a certain resemblance between the two essays.* **4.** In confidence restricted to: *Between you and me, he is not qualified.* **5a.** By the combined effort or effect of: *"Sickly, it began to occur to him that between them, they might have killed the old man by mistake"* (Jane Stevenson, *London Bridges*). **b.** In the combined ownership of: *They had only a few dollars between them.* **6.** As measured or compared against: *"[She] went to the butcher's to choose between steak and pork chops"* (Sinclar Lewis, *Main Street*).

adverb

In an intermediate space, position, or time; in the interim.

IDIOM:

in between In an intermediate condition or situation: *"The methane, however, cannot exist in its normal* *gaseous form at such pressures and temperatures, but is transformed into a 'supercritical fluid'—neither a gas nor a liquid but something in between*" (Malcolm W. Browne, *New York Times*).

[Middle English *bitwene,* from Old English *betwēonum.*]

RELATED WORD:

noun—**be·tween′ness**

❧ The *-tween* in *between* comes from the same Indo-European root that gave us *two, twain,* and *duo,* and the *-mong* of *among* comes from an Old English word that meant "crowd" or "throng." It is thus unsurprising that a traditional rule requires *between* to be used only for sentences involving two items and *among* for sentences involving more than two. Indeed, in sentences involving two items, no rule is needed; native English speakers spontaneously use *between* (as in *the differences between* [not *among*] *karate and judo*). But when there are more than two items, practice is mixed. Many careful writers observe a more subtle distinction, using *among* when the sentence refers to the entities collectively or as a mass, as in *There were many outstanding players among the teams in the quarterfinal round* or *A thistle is growing among the roses,* but preferring *between* when the sentence refers to relationships involving particular pairs of entities from within the group, as in *We haven't yet assigned the matchups between teams in the quarterfinal round* or *I have sand between my toes.* In such sentences, the twoness of *between* has not, so to speak, been lost in the crowd—the pairings within the larger group are important to the meaning of the sentence and thus influence the writer's choice of preposition.

15

bla·tant (blāt′nt)

adjective

1. Unpleasantly loud and noisy: *"There are those who find the trombones blatant and the triangle silly, but both add effective color"* (Musical Heritage Review). **2.** USAGE PROBLEM Thoroughly or offensively conspicuous or obtrusive: *The child was caught telling a blatant lie.*

[From Latin *blatīre,* to blab (on the model of words such as *rampant*).]

RELATED WORDS:

noun—**bla′tan·cy**
adverb—**bla′tant·ly**

Blatant and *flagrant* both attribute conspicuousness and offensiveness to certain acts, but the words differ in emphasis. *Blatant* means "offensively conspicuous," and thus emphasizes the actor's failure to conceal the act. *Flagrant,* on the other hand, means "conspicuously offensive," and emphasizes the serious wrongdoing inherent in the offense. Thus many actions, from an infraction of the rules in a football game to a violation of human rights, may be *blatant* or *flagrant,* depending on what is being emphasized. If the act is committed with contempt for public scrutiny, it is *blatant.* If the act seems extreme in its violation of norms, it is *flagrant.*

Blatant and (to a much lesser extent) *flagrant* are sometimes used as synonyms of *obvious,* in contexts where there is no immediate connection to human behavior, as in *What surprised us was that they went ahead with the idea in spite of the blatant danger of the approach.* This usage has traditionally been considered an error, and it is not surprising, therefore, that most of the Usage Panel dislikes it. In our 2004 survey, only 42 percent accepted the sentence just listed.

16

cap·i·tal (kăp′ĭ-tl)

noun

1a. A town or city that is the official seat of government in a political entity, such as a state or nation: *Trenton is the capital of New Jersey.* **b.** A city that is the center of a specific activity or industry: *Many consider Milan to be the fashion capital of the world.* **2a.** Wealth in the form of money or property that is used or accumulated in a business by a person, partnership, or corporation, and is often used to create more wealth. **b.** Human resources considered in terms of their contributions to an economy: *"Castro's swift unveiling of his communist plans provoked a flight of human capital"* (George F. Will, *Newsweek*). **3.** The remaining assets of a business after all liabilities have been deducted; net worth. **4a.** The total amount of stock authorized for issue by a corporation, including common and preferred stock. **b.** The total stated or par value of the permanently invested capital of a corporation. **5.** An asset or advantage: *"He has profited from political capital accumulated by others"* (Michael Mandelbaum, *Foreign Affairs*). **6.** A capital letter.

adjective

1. First and foremost; principal: *We were faced with a decision of capital importance.* **2.** First-rate; excellent: *Planning a kayaking trip is a capital idea!* **3.** Relating to or being a seat of government: *Albany, New York, is a capital city.* **4.** Punishable by or involving death: *Treason is a capital offense.* **5.** Of or involving wealth and its use in investment: *"A multi-billion-dollar capital improvement plan has produced construction, physical im-*

provements, and repairs" (Peter Edelman, *Searching for America's Heart*).

[From Middle English, principal, from Old French, from Latin *capitālis*, from *caput*, head, money laid out.]

✎ *Capital* and *capitol* are terms that are often confused, mainly because they refer to things that are in some way related. The term for a town or city that serves as a seat of government is spelled *capital*. The term for the building in which a legislative assembly meets is spelled *capitol*.

17

cap·i·tol (kăp′ĭ-tl)

noun

1. A building or complex of buildings in which a state legislature meets. **2. Capitol** The building in Washington DC where the Congress of the United States meets.

[Middle English *Capitol*, Jupiter's temple in Rome, from Old French *capitole*, from Latin *Capitōlium*, after *Capitōlīnus*, Capitoline, the hill on which Jupiter's temple stood; perhaps akin to *caput*; see etymology at **capital** (#16).]

SEE NOTE AT **capital** (# 16).

"The Pyncheon Elm, throughout its great circumference, was all alive, and full of the morning sun and a sweet-tempered little breeze, which lingered within this verdant sphere, and set a thousand leafy tongues a-whispering all at once. This aged tree appeared to have suffered nothing from the gale. It had kept its boughs unshattered, and its full **complement** of leaves; and the whole in perfect verdure, except a single branch, that, by the earlier change with which the elm-tree sometimes prophesies the autumn, had been transmuted to bright gold."

—Nathaniel Hawthorne,
The House of the Seven Gables

18

com·ple·ment (kŏm′plə-mənt)

noun

1a. Something that completes, makes up a whole, or brings to perfection. **b.** The quantity or number needed to make up a whole: "[The tree] *had kept its boughs unshattered, and its full complement of leaves* (Nathaniel Hawthorne, *The House of the Seven Gables*). **c.** Either of two parts that complete the whole or mutually complete each other. **2.** An angle related to another so that the sum of their measures is 90°. **3.** A word or words used after a verb to complete a predicate construction; for example, the phrase *to eat ice cream* is the complement of the predicate *We like to eat ice cream.* **4.** A complex system of proteins found in normal blood plasma that combines with antibodies to destroy pathogenic bacteria and other foreign cells.

transitive verb (kŏm′plə-mĕnt′)

Past participle and past tense: **com·ple·ment·ed**
Present participle: **com·ple·ment·ing**
Third person singular present tense: **com·ple·ments**

To serve as a complement to: "*When chiles are dried, their flavor intensifies, and sometimes they take on a smoky, sweet flavor that complements the heat*" (Corby Kummer, *Atlantic Monthly*).

[Middle English, from Old French, from Latin *complēmentum,* from *complēre,* to fill out.]

Complement and *compliment,* though quite distinct in meaning, are sometimes confused because they are pronounced the same. As a noun, *complement* means "something that completes or brings to perfection" *(The antique silver was a complement to the beautifully set table)*; used as a verb it means "to serve as a complement to" (*The neutral color of the paint complements the warmth of the oak floors*). The noun *compliment* means "an expression or act of courtesy or praise" *(They gave us a compliment on our beautifully set table)*, while the verb means "to pay a compliment to" (*We complimented our hosts for the lovely dinner party*).

19

com·pli·ment (kŏm′plə-mənt)

noun

1. An expression of praise, admiration, or congratulation: *I took their interest in my screenplay as a compliment.* **2.** A formal act of civility, courtesy, or respect: *"You must give me leave to judge for myself, and pay me the compliment of believing what I say"* (Jane Austen, *Pride and Prejudice*). **3. compliments** Good wishes; regards: *Extend my compliments to your parents.*

transitive verb

Past participle and past tense: **com·pli·ment·ed**
Present participle: **com·pli·ment·ing**
Third person singular present tense: **com·pli·ments**

To pay a compliment to: *The mayor complimented the volunteers who had cleaned up the park.*

[French, from Italian *complimento,* from Spanish *cumplimiento,* from *cumplir,* to complete, from Latin *complēre,* to fill out.]

SEE NOTE AT **complement** (# 18).

20

com·prise (kəm-prīz′)

transitive verb

Past participle and past tense: **com·prised**
Present participle: **com·pris·ing**
Third person singular present tense: **com·pris·es**

1. To consist of; be composed of: *"The French got what became known as French Equatorial Africa, comprising several territories"* (Alex Shoumatoff, *Vanity Fair*). **2.** To include; contain: *"The word 'politics' . . . comprises, in itself, a difficult study of no inconsiderable magnitude"* (Charles Dickens, *The Pickwick Papers*). **3.** USAGE PROBLEM To compose; constitute.

[Middle English *comprisen,* from Old French *compris*, past participle of *comprendre*, to include, from Latin *comprehendere, comprēndere.*]

☙ The traditional rule states that the whole *comprises* the parts and the parts *compose* the whole. In strict usage: *The Union comprises 50 states. Fifty states compose* (or *make up*) *the Union.* Even though many writers maintain this distinction, *comprise* is often used in place of *compose,* especially in the passive: *The Union is comprised of 50 states.* Our surveys show that opposition to this usage has abated but has not disappeared. In the 1960s, 53 percent of the Usage Panel found this usage unacceptable; by 1996, the proportion objecting had declined to 35 percent; and by 2011, it had fallen a bit more, to 32 percent.

21 **con·sul** (kŏn′səl)

noun

1. An official appointed by a government to reside in a foreign country and represent his or her government's commercial interests and assist its citizens there. **2.** Either of the two chief magistrates of the Roman Republic, elected for a term of one year. **3.** Any of the three chief magistrates of the French Republic from 1799 to 1804.

[Middle English *consul,* Roman consul, from Latin *cōnsul;* possibly akin to *cōnsulere,* to take counsel.]

RELATED WORDS:

adjective—**con′su·lar** (kŏn′sə-lər)
noun—**con′sul·ship′**

SEE NOTE AT **council** (# 23).

22 **con·vince** (kən-vĭns′)

transitive verb

Past participle and past tense: **con·vinced**
Present participle: **con·vinc·ing**
Third person singular present tense: **con·vinc·es**

To bring by the use of argument or evidence to firm belief or a course of action: *"I was now quite convinced that she had made a fresh will, and had called the two gardeners in to witness her signature. Events proved that I was right in my supposition"* (Agatha Christie, *The Mysterious Affair at Styles*).

[Latin *convincere,* to prove wrong : *com-*, intensive prefix + *vincere,* to conquer.]

RELATED WORDS:

noun—**con·vinc′er**
adjective—**con·vinc′i·ble**

According to a traditional rule, one *persuades* someone to act but *convinces* someone of the truth of a statement or proposition: *By convincing me that no good could come of staying, he persuaded me to leave.* If the distinction is accepted, then *convince* should not be used with an infinitive: He *persuaded* (not *convinced*) me to go. In a 1981 Usage Panel survey, 61 percent rejected the use of *convince* with an infinitive. But the tide of sentiment against the construction appears to be turning. In a 1996 survey, 74 percent accepted it in the sentence *I tried to convince him to chip in a few dollars, but he refused.* Even in passive constructions, a majority of the Usage Panel accepted *convince* with an infinitive. Fifty-two percent accepted the sentence *After listening to the teacher's report, the committee was convinced to go ahead with the new reading program. Persuade,* on the other hand, is perfectly acceptable when used with an infinitive or a *that* clause in both active and passive constructions. An overwhelming majority of Panelists in the 1996 survey accepted the following sentences: *After a long discussion with her lawyer, she was persuaded to drop the lawsuit. The President persuaded his advisors that military action was necessary.* You can observe the traditional distinction between these words, but it is not very likely that readers will appreciate the effort.

23 coun·cil (koun′səl)

noun

1a. An assembly of persons called together for consultation, deliberation, or discussion. **b.** A body of people elected or appointed to serve as administrators, legislators, or advisors. **c.** An assembly of church officials and theologians convened for regulating matters of doctrine and discipline. **2.** The discussion or deliberation that takes place in such an assembly or body.

[Middle English *counceil,* from Old French *concile,* from Latin.]

Council, counsel, and *consul* have similar pronunciations but are never interchangeable, although their meanings are related. *Council* refers principally to a deliberative assembly (such as a city council or student council), its work, and its membership. *Counsel* pertains chiefly to advice and guidance in general and to a person (such as a lawyer or camp counselor) who provides it. *Consul* denotes an officer in the foreign service of a country.

24 coun·sel (koun′səl)

noun

1. The act of exchanging opinions and ideas; consultation: *Frequent counsel among the members kept the committee informed.* **2.** Advice or guidance, especially as solicited from a knowledgeable person: "*I wish to engage your keener faculties, your logic and reason, so that you are able to discern a greater truth than I can. In short, I seek counsel and instruction*" (*Audubon's Watch,* John Gregory Brown). **3.** Private, guarded thoughts or opinions: *The quiet loner always kept his own counsel.* **4.** A lawyer or group of lawyers giving legal advice and especially conducting a case in court.

verb

Past participle and past tense: **coun·seled** *or* **coun·selled**

Present participle: **coun·sel·ing** *or* **coun·sel·ling**

Third person singular present tense: **coun·sels**

transitive **1.** To give counsel to; advise: *"An Owl, in her wisdom, counseled the Birds that when the acorn first began to sprout, to pull it all up out of the ground and not allow it to grow"* (Aesop, *Fables: The Owl and the Birds*). **2.** To recommend: *counseled care in the forthcoming negotiations.*

intransitive To give or take advice.

[Middle English *counseil,* from Old French *conseil,* from Latin *cōnsilium*; akin to *cōnsulere,* to take counsel, consult.]

RELATED WORDS:

noun—**coun′sel·or, coun′sel·lor**
noun—**coun′sel·or·ship′**

SEE NOTE AT **council** (# 23).

25

dis·creet (dĭ-skrēt′)

adjective

Marked by, exercising, or showing prudence and wise self-restraint in speech and behavior; circumspect: *"After-hours clubs are proliferating and are still the city's best-kept secrets. One need only make discreet inquiries as to the whereabouts of such places"* (Doris Pike, *Boston Magazine)*.

[Middle English, from Old French *discret,* from Medieval Latin *discrētus,* from Latin, past participle of *discernere,* to separate, discern.]

RELATED WORDS:

adverb—**dis·creet′ly**
noun—**dis·creet′ness**

SEE NOTE AT **discrete** (# 26).

26

dis·crete (dĭ-skrēt′)

adjective

Constituting a separate thing: *"Although hypertext may well turn out to be no more than an amusing detour in the history of the written word, its most ardent fans foresee a future in which traditional narratives would become obsolete, and discrete, self-contained books would also give way to vast interlinked electronic networks"* (Michiko Kakutani, *New York Times Magazine*).

[Middle English, from Old French, from Latin *discrētus,* past participle of *discernere,* to separate.]

RELATED WORDS:

adverb—**dis·crete′ly**
noun—**dis·crete′ness**

Because they are pronounced the same way, *discreet* and *discrete* are sometimes confused in print. *Discreet* means "prudent in speech and behavior": *He told me the news but asked me to be discreet about it.* The related word *discrete* means "separate, distinct": *The summer science program consists of four discrete units.*

27

dis·in·ter·est·ed (dĭs-ĭn′trĭ-stĭd, dĭs-ĭn′tə-rĕs′tĭd)

adjective

1. Free of bias and self-interest; impartial: *"Debates on the fluoridation issue are passionate and polemical. For this reason disinterested scientific opinion on fluorides in the water supply, which is itself hard to come by, is not always the basis for public policy"* (Ellen R. Shell, *Atlantic Monthly*). **2.** USAGE PROBLEM Not interested or having lost interest; indifferent.

RELATED WORDS:

adverb—**dis·in′ter·est·ed·ly**
noun—**dis·in′ter·est·ed·ness**

In traditional usage, *disinterested* can only mean "having no stake in an outcome," as in *Since the judge stands to profit from the sale of the company, she cannot be considered a disinterested party in the dispute.* This usage was acceptable to 98 percent of the Usage Panel in our 2013 survey. But despite critical disapproval, *disinterested* has come to be widely used to mean "uninterested" or "having lost interest," as in *Since she discovered skiing, she's become disinterested in ice skating.* The "not interested" meaning is actually the oldest sense of the word, going back to the 1600s. Despite its pedigree, this usage began to be considered an error in the 1900s. In five surveys spanning almost fifty years, the Usage Panel has consistently disapproved of sentences that use *disinterested* to mean "uninterested." In our 2013 survey, for example, 86 percent of the Usage Panel found the sentence *It is difficult to imagine an approach better designed to prevent disinterested students from developing any intellectual maturity* to be unacceptable. This figure is essentially unchanged from the 88 percent of the Panel that disapproved of the same sentence in 2001.

ef·fect (ĭ-fĕkt′)

noun

1. Something brought about by a cause or agent; a result: *"Every cause produces more than one effect"* (Herbert Spencer, *Essays on Education*). **2.** The power to produce an outcome or achieve a result; influence: *The drug had an immediate effect on the pain. The government's action had no effect on the trade imbalance.* **3.** A scientific law, hypothesis, or phenomenon: *the photovoltaic effect.* **4.** Advantage; avail: *The lawyer used the words of the witness to great effect in influencing the jury.* **5.** The condition of being in full force or execution: *This new regulation goes into effect on January 1.* **6a.** Something that produces a specific impression or supports a general design or intention: *The strange lighting effects emphasized the harsh atmosphere of the drama.* **b.** A particular impression: *These large windows give an effect of spaciousness.* **c.** Production of a desired impression: *spent lavishly on dinner just for effect.* **7.** The basic or general meaning; import: *He said he was greatly worried, or words to that effect.* **8. effects** Movable belongings; goods.

transitive verb

Past participle and past tense: **ef·fect·ed**
Present participle: **ef·fect·ing**
Third person singular present tense: **ef·fects**

To produce as a result; cause to occur: *"It is known that the English pointer has been greatly changed within the last century, and in this case the change has, it is believed, been chiefly effected by crosses with the fox*" (Charles Darwin, *On the Origin of Species*).

IDIOM:

in effect In essence; to all purposes: *testimony that in effect contradicted her earlier statement.*

[Middle English, from Old French, from Latin *effectus,* from past participle of *efficere,* to accomplish : *ex-,* ex- + *facere,* to make.]

RELATED WORDS:

noun—**ef·fect′er**
adjective—**ef·fect′i·ble**

✍ The words *affect* and *effect* are often confused, in no small part because they often sound the same. What's worse, two different words are spelled *affect.* One is solely a verb and means "to put on a false show of," as in *The actor affected a British accent.* The other can be both a noun and a verb. The noun meaning "emotion" is a technical term from psychology that sometimes shows up in general writing, as in the quote "*The soldiers seen on television had been carefully chosen for blandness of affect*" written by Norman Mailer in a piece about the Gulf War. In its far more common role as a verb, *affect* usually means "to influence," as in *The Surgeon General's report outlined how much smoking affects health.*

Effect can also serve as a noun or a verb. The noun means "a result." Thus, if you *affect* something, you are likely to see an *effect* of some kind, and from this may arise further the confusion. As a verb, *effect* means "to bring about or execute." Thus, using *effect* in the sentence *These measures may effect savings* implies that the measures will cause new savings to come about. But using *affect* in the very similar sentence *These measures may affect savings* could just as easily imply that the measures may reduce savings that have already been realized.

29 **en·er·vate** (ĕn′ər-vāt′)

transitive verb

Past participle and past tense: **en·er·vat·ed**
Present participle: **en·er·vat·ing**
Third person singular present tense: **en·er·vates**

1. To weaken or destroy the strength or vitality of: "*What is the nature of the luxury which enervates and destroys nations?*" (Henry David Thoreau, *Walden*). **2.** In medicine, to remove a nerve or part of a nerve.

[Latin *ēnervāre, ēnervāt-* : *ē-*, *ex-*, ex- + *nervus,* sinew.]

RELATED WORDS:

noun—**en′er·va′tion**
adjective—**en′er·va′tive**
noun—**en′er·va′tor**

By mistakenly assuming that *enervate* is a close cousin of the verb *energize,* people sometimes use *enervate* incorrectly to mean "to invigorate" or "to excite" (as in *I was sleepy, so I took a cold shower hoping it would enervate me*). In fact, *enervate* does not come from the same source as *energize* (Greek *energos,* "active"). It comes from Latin *nervus,* "sinew." Thus *enervate* means "to cause to become 'out of muscle'," that is, "to weaken or deplete of strength."

e·nor·mi·ty (ĭ-nôr′mĭ-tē)

noun

Plural: **e·nor·mi·ties**

1. The quality of passing all moral bounds; excessive wickedness or outrageousness. **2.** A monstrous offense or evil; an outrage. **3.** USAGE PROBLEM Great size; immensity: *The enormity of the hot-air balloon amazed all the onlookers.*

[French *énormité,* from Old French, from Latin *ēnormitās,* from *ēnormis,* unusual, enormous.]

Enormity is frequently used to refer simply to the property of being great in size or extent, but many would prefer that *enormousness* (or a synonym such as *immensity*) be used for this general sense and that *enormity* be limited to situations that demand a negative moral judgment, as in *Not until the war ended and journalists were able to enter Cambodia did the world really become aware of the enormity of Pol Pot's oppression.* According to this rule, the sentence *At that point, the engineers sat down to design an entirely new viaduct, apparently undaunted by the enormity of their task* would be considered incorrect. This distinction between *enormity* and *enormousness* has not always existed historically, but nowadays many observe it. You may want to avoid using *enormity* in phrases such as *the enormity of the support the mayor received in the election* as *enormity*'s sense of monstrousness may leave your audience misinterpreting what it is you are trying to say.

31 **e·nor·mous·ness** (ĭ-nôr′məs-nəs)

noun

The state or condition of being very great in size, extent, number, or degree: "[The whale] *seemed hardly to budge at all . . . good evidence was hereby furnished of the enormousness of the mass we moved*" (Herman Melville, *Moby-Dick*).

[*enormous* (from Latin *ēnormis,* unusual, huge, monstrous : *ē-, ex-,* ex- + *norma,* norm) + *-ness* (from Middle English *-nes,* from Old English).]

RELATED WORDS:

adjective—**e·nor′mous**
adverb—**e·nor′mous·ly**

SEE NOTE AT **enormity** (# 30).

32

en·sure (ĕn-sho͝or′)

transitive verb

Past participle and past tense: **en·sured**
Present participle: **en·sur·ing**
Third person singular present tense: **en·sures**

To make sure or certain; insure: "*The world is still engaged in a massive armaments race designed to ensure continuing equivalent strength among potential adversaries*" (Jimmy Carter, Inaugural Address).

[Middle English *ensuren,* from Anglo-Norman *enseurer* : Old French *en-*, causative prefix + Old French *seur,* secure, variant of *sur.*]

SEE NOTE AT **insure** (# 49).

"The world is still engaged in a massive armaments race designed to **ensure** continuing equivalent strength among potential adversaries. We pledge perseverance and wisdom in our efforts to limit the world's armaments to those necessary for each nation's own domestic safety. And we will move this year a step toward our ultimate goal—the elimination of all nuclear weapons from this Earth. We urge all other people to join us, for success can mean life instead of death."

—Jimmy Carter,
Inaugural Address

33

fac·toid (făk′toid)

noun

1. A piece of unverified or inaccurate information that is presented in the press as factual, often as part of a publicity effort, and that is then accepted as true because of frequent repetition: *"What one misses finally is what might have emerged beyond both facts and factoids—a profound definition of the Marilyn Monroe phenomenon"* (Christopher Lehmann-Haupt, *New York Times*). **2.** USAGE PROBLEM A brief, somewhat interesting fact.

RELATED WORD:

adjective—**fac·toi′dal**

The suffix *-oid* normally means "resembling, having the appearance of." Thus, *factoid* originally referred to a claim that appears reliable or accurate, often because it has been repeated so frequently that people assume it is true. The word still has this meaning for many writers and readers; in our 2013 survey, 59 percent of the Usage Panel accepted it in the sentence *The editorial writer relied on numerous factoids that have long been discredited.* But *factoid* is also often used to mean a brief, somewhat interesting fact, and this sense has become common in recent decades. Some 64 percent of the Panel accepted this usage in the sentence *Each issue of the magazine begins with a list of factoids, like how many pounds of hamburger were consumed in Texas last month.* As the ballot results indicate, neither usage is overwhelmingly approved. If you use the word *factoid*, be sure the sentence makes it clear whether you are referring to a spurious claim, on the one hand, or an isolated, trivial, or mildly intriguing fact, on the other.

34

few·er (fyo͞o′ər)

adjective

The comparative form of **few.** Amounting to or consisting of a smaller number: *The catcher played fewer innings than the shortstop did.*

pronoun

A smaller number of persons or things: *Chris ate six slices of pizza, and Lee had fewer.*

[Middle English, from Old English *fēawe* + Middle English *-er,* comparative suffix.]

☙ The traditional rule holds that *fewer* should be used for things that can be counted (*fewer than four players*), while *less* should be used with mass nouns for things of measurable extent (*less paper; less than a gallon of paint*). The Usage Panel largely supports the traditional rule. In our 2006 survey, only five percent accepted the sentence *There are less crowds at the mall these days,* while 28 percent accepted the following sentence, in which *less* is contrasted with *more*: *The region needs more jobs, not less jobs.* The Panel was a little more accepting (but still not in favor) of the familiar supermarket usage *The express lane is reserved for shoppers with 10 or less items.* The traditional rule is often hard to follow in practice, however, in part because plural nouns and mass nouns are similar in being divisible and in lacking distinct boundaries. For this reason, plurals and mass nouns are used in many of the same ways. Both can be used without determiners (*I like apples, I like applesauce*), and they both can take certain quantifiers like *some* and *more* (*more apples, more applesauce*). *Less* falls in the same class as *some* and *more* and is used in some well-established constructions where *fewer* would occur if the traditional rule were applied. *Less than* can be used before a plural noun that denotes a measure of time, amount, or distance: *less than three weeks; less than $400; less than 50 miles.*

Less is sometimes used with plural nouns in the expressions *no less than* (as in *No less than 30 of his colleagues signed the letter*) and *or less* (as in *Give your reasons in 25 words or less*). And the approximator *more or less* is normally used after plural nouns as well as mass nouns: *I have two dozen apples, more or less.* To use *fewer* in such constructions sounds fastidious, so writers who follow the traditional rule should do so with caution.

35 **fla·grant** (flā′grənt)

adjective

Conspicuously bad, offensive, or reprehensible: "*[S]ometimes the very presence of received wisdom keeps blinders on us all, even when evidence of abuse of power or sloppy procedures is flagrant*" (Patricia Holt, *San Francisco Chronicle*).

[Latin *flagrāns, flagrant-*, present participle of *flagrāre*, to burn.]

RELATED WORDS:

noun—**fla′grance**
adverb—**fla′grant·ly**

SEE NOTE AT **blatant** (# 15).

36 **flam·ma·ble** (flăm′ə-bəl)

adjective

Easily ignited and capable of burning rapidly; inflammable: "*Until the early 1980's, many renderers had used flammable solvents to dissolve fats, and the solvents may have deactivated the agent that causes mad cow disease and scrapie*" (Sandra Blakeslee, *New York Times*).

[From Latin *flammāre,* to set fire to, from *flamma,* flame.]

RELATED WORDS:

noun—**flam′ma·bil′i·ty**
noun—**flam′ma·ble**
adverb—**flam′ma·bly**

SEE NOTE AT **inflammable** (# 48).

37 **flaunt** (flônt)

verb

Past participle and past tense: **flaunt·ed**
Present participle: **flaunt·ing**
Third person singular present tense: **flaunts**

transitive **1.** To exhibit ostentatiously or shamelessly: "*In everything a prudent man acts with knowledge, but a fool flaunts his folly*" (Proverbs 13:16). **2.** USAGE PROBLEM To show contempt for; scorn.

intransitive **1.** To parade oneself ostentatiously; show oneself off. **2.** To wave grandly: "*Flaunt away, flags of all nations!*" (Walt Whitman, *Leaves of Grass).*

[Origin unknown.]

RELATED WORDS:

noun—**flaunt′er**
adverb—**flaunt′ing·ly**

Flaunt as a transitive verb means "to exhibit ostentatiously": *She flaunted her wealth.* To *flout* is "to show contempt for something by disregarding it": *Some people at the reception flouted convention by wearing sneakers.* For some time now *flaunt* has been used in the sense "to show contempt for," even by educated users of English. But this usage is still widely seen as erroneous. In our 2009 survey, 73 percent of the Usage Panel rejected it in the sentence *This is just another example of an executive flaunting the rules for personal gain.*

38

flout (flout)

verb

Past participle and past tense: **flout·ed**
Present participle: **flout·ing**
Third person singular present tense: **flouts**

transitive To show contempt for; scorn: *"Considered on its face, suicide flouts the laws of nature, slashing through the sturdy instinct that wills all beings to fight for their lives until they can fight no longer"* (Natalie Angier, *The Beauty of the Beastly*).

intransitive To be scornful.

noun

A contemptuous action or remark; an insult: *"Bruise me with scorn, confound me with a flout; / Thrust thy sharp wit quite through my ignorance; / Cut me to pieces with thy keen conceit"* (William Shakespeare, *Love's Labours Lost*).

RELATED WORDS:

noun—**flout′er**
adverb—**flout′ing·ly**

[Perhaps from Middle English *flouten,* to play the flute, from Old French *flauter,* from *flaute,* flute.]

SEE NOTE AT **flaunt** (# 37).

39

for·te (fôr′tā′, fôrt)

noun

1. Something in which a person excels: *"[O]ur senator had the misfortune to be a man who had a particularly humane and accessible nature, and turning away anybody that was in trouble never had been his forte"* (Harriet Beecher Stowe, *Uncle Tom's Cabin*). **2.** The strong part of a sword blade, between the middle and the hilt.

[French *fort,* from Old French, strong, from Latin *fortis.*]

Many claim that the word *forte,* coming from French *fort,* should properly be pronounced with one syllable, like the English word *fort.* Common usage, however, prefers the two-syllable pronunciation, (fôr′tā′), which has been influenced possibly by the music term *forte,* borrowed from Italian. Speakers can continue to pronounce it as one syllable knowing that the origin of the word supports this pronunciation, but they do so at an increasing risk of puzzling their listeners.

gen·der (jĕn′dər)

noun

1a. A grammatical category used in the classification of nouns, pronouns, adjectives, and, in some languages, verbs that may be arbitrary or based on characteristics such as sex or animacy and that determines agreement with or selection of modifiers, referents, or grammatical forms. **b.** The distinguishing form or forms used. **2.** Sexual identity, especially in relation to society or culture. **3a.** The condition of being female or male; sex. **b.** Females or males considered as a group: *The linguist studied expressions predominantly used by one gender.*

[Middle English *gendre,* from Old French, kind, gender, from Latin *genus, gener-*.]

Traditionally, *gender* has been used primarily to refer to the grammatical categories of "masculine," "feminine," and "neuter," but in recent years the word has become well established in its use to refer to sex-based categories, as in phrases such as *gender gap* and *the politics of gender.* This usage is supported by the practice of many anthropologists and others concerned with the behaviors and attitudes of men and women. This distinction is sometimes summed up by the expression "Sex is who we are; gender is what we do." Accordingly, one would say *The effectiveness of the medication appears to depend on the sex* (not *gender*) *of the patient,* but *In peasant societies, gender* (not *sex*) *roles are likely to be more clearly defined.* This distinction is useful in principle, but it is by no means widely observed, and considerable variation in usage occurs at all levels.

41

hope·ful·ly (hōp′fə-lē)

adverb

1. In a hopeful manner. **2.** USAGE PROBLEM It is to be hoped: *Hopefully, it will stop raining before the game starts.*

"Hopefully, the senator will vote for the bill." Is this sentence saying that one hopes the senator will vote a certain way? Or is it declaring that when the senator votes, it will be done in a hopeful manner? In the first case, the word modifies the entire sentence (functioning as what is known as a sentence adverb) and means "It is to be hoped." In the second case, it modifies the verb phrase "will vote" and means "in a hopeful manner." Since the 1960s, when *hopefully* became something of a vogue word, its use as a sentence adverb has been roundly criticized on the grounds that it can be ambiguous (which meaning is intended?) and that the bearer of hope is not explicitly indicated (who is hopeful)? It is unclear, however, why *hopefully* was singled out for criticism. Many other adverbs, such as *mercifully* and *frankly,* are regularly used as sentence adverbs: *Mercifully, the play was brief. Frankly, the food at that restaurant is terrible.* The widespread use of *hopefully* in similar constructions reflects popular recognition of its usefulness; there is no precise substitute. Someone who says *Hopefully, the treaty will be ratified* makes a hopeful prediction about the fate of the treaty, whereas someone who says *I hope* (or *We hope* or *It is hoped that*) *the treaty will be ratified* expresses a bald statement about what is desired. Only the latter could be continued with a clause such as *but it isn't likely.*

People often warm to a usage once its novelty fades and it becomes well established. Resistance to this usage has waned over the years, but the gradual path to acceptance has taken much longer than other style choices that were bugbears in the 1960s, such as using *impact* or *contact* as verbs. In 1999, 34 percent of the Usage Panel accepted the sentence *Hopefully, the treaty will be ratified.* In 2012, 63 percent accepted this same sentence. But a significantly larger percentage—89 percent—accepted a comparable use of *mercifully* in 2012, indicating that it is not the use of *hopefully* as a sentence adverb per se that bothers the Panel. Rather, *hopefully* appears to be serving as a shibboleth to reveal whether a speaker is aware of the traditional canons of usage.

42

im·pact (ĭm′păkt′)

noun

1. The striking of one body against another; collision: *The impact of the meteorite left a large crater.* **2.** The effect or impression of one thing on another: *The report gauges the impact of automation on the lives of factory workers.* **3.** The power of making a strong, immediate impression: *Unfortunately, the candidate gave a speech that lacked impact.*

verb (ĭm-păkt′)

Past participle and past tense: **im·pact·ed**
Present participle: **im·pact·ing**
Third person singular present tense: **im·pacts**

transitive **1.** To pack firmly together. **2.** To strike forcefully: *The astronomers observed meteorites impacting the lunar surface.* **3.** USAGE PROBLEM To have an effect or impact on: *The manufacturing industry has been impacted by recent trade agreements.*

intransitive USAGE PROBLEM To have an effect or impact.

[From Latin *impāctus*, past participle of *impingere*, to push against.]

RELATED WORD:

noun—**im·pac′tion**

☞ The use of *impact* as a verb meaning "to have an effect" often has a big impact on readers. Most language critics disapprove of the construction *to impact on*, as in *These policies are impacting on our ability to achieve success*, a sentence 85 percent of the Usage Panel found unacceptable in 2001. The use of *impact* as a transitive verb, as in the sentence *The court ruling will impact the education of minority students*, was unacceptable to 80 percent of the Panel.

It is unclear why this usage provokes such a strong response, but it cannot be because of novelty. *Impact* has been used as a verb since 1601, when it meant "to fix or pack in," and its modern, figurative use dates from 1935. It may be that its frequent appearance in the jargon-riddled remarks of politicians, military officials, and financial analysts continues to make people suspicious. Nevertheless, the verbal use of *impact* has become so common in the working language of corporations and institutions that many speakers have begun to regard it as standard.

43

im·peach (ĭm-pēch′)

transitive verb

Past participle and past tense: **im·peached**
Present participle: **im·peach·ing**
Third person singular present tense: **im·peach·es**

1. To charge (a public official) with improper conduct in office before a proper tribunal: *The House of Representatives impeached Andrew Johnson in 1868 and Bill Clinton in 1998; neither was convicted.* **2.** To challenge the validity of; try to discredit: *The lawyer impeached the witness's credibility with a string of damaging questions.*

[Middle English *empechen*, to impede, accuse, from Anglo-Norman *empecher*, from Late Latin *impedicāre*, to entangle : Latin *in-*, in + Latin *pedica*, fetter.]

RELATED WORDS:

adjective—**im·peach′a·ble**
noun—**im·peach′er**
noun—**im·peach′ment**

When an irate citizen demands that a disfavored public official be impeached, the citizen clearly intends for the official to be removed from office. This popular use of *impeach* as a synonym of "throw out" (even if by due process) does not accord with the legal meaning of the word. As recent history has shown, when a public official is impeached, that is, formally accused of wrongdoing, this is only the start of what can be a lengthy process that may or may not lead to the official's removal from office. In strict usage, an official is impeached (accused), tried, and then convicted or acquitted. The vaguer use of *impeach* reflects disgruntled citizens' indifference to whether the official is forced from office by legal means or chooses to resign to avoid further disgrace.

44 im·ply (ĭm-plī′)

transitive verb

Past participle and past tense: **im·plied**
Present participle: **im·ply·ing**
Third person singular present tense: **im·plies**

1. To involve by logical necessity; entail: "*[S]chool would be a complete change: it implied a long journey, an entire separation from Gateshead, an entrance into a new life*" (Charlotte Brontë, *Jane Eyre*). **2.** To express or indicate indirectly: "*'Oh, shut up!' murmured his brother Dan. The manner of his words implied that this fraternal voice near him was an indescribable bore*" (Stephen Crane, *The Little Regiment*).

[Middle English *implien,* from Old French *emplier,* to enfold, from Latin *implicāre.*]

SEE NOTE AT **infer** (# 47).

45

in·cred·i·ble (ĭn-krĕd′ə-bəl)

adjective

1. So implausible as to elicit disbelief: "*The next instant we were flying headlong through the air toward the surface of the lake a hundred feet below. Men have told me since that I never made that dive, or that I greatly overestimated the distance, and I admit that as I look back at it now it appears incredible*" (Rex Stout, *Under The Andes*). **2.** Extraordinary: "*My father . . . became a busker and then a singing waiter and then a songwriter, and he felt incredible gratitude to this country for giving him the chance to become who he became*" (Mary Ellin Barrett, *Newsweek*).

[Middle English, from Latin *incrēdibilis* : *in-*, not + *crēdibilis*, believable.]

RELATED WORDS:

noun—**in·cred′i·bil′i·ty**
noun—**in·cred′i·ble·ness**
adverb—**in·cred′i·bly**

☙ *Incredible* means "hard to believe, unbelievable": *His explanation of the cause of the accident was simply incredible.* It is often used more loosely to mean "extraordinary" or "astonishing," as in *The new pitcher has an incredible fastball. Incredulous* usually means "skeptical, disbelieving," as in *The incredulous reporters laughed at the manager's explanation of how the funds disappeared.* It is sometimes extended to mean "showing disbelief," as in *an incredulous stare.* You may occasionally see *incredulous* used where you would expect *incredible,* as in *an incredulous display of rudeness.* This usage is not well established, however, and is widely considered an error.

46

in·cred·u·lous (ĭn-krĕj′ə-ləs)

adjective

1. Disbelieving or doubtful; skeptical: *"[B]efore me the ice parted to reveal the cold, muddy swirl twisting below. . . . That's when common sense and terror hit and I headed for shore. . . . When I reached land, I looked back, incredulous that I'd thought I could actually make it across"* (William Least Heat-Moon, *River-Horse*). **2.** Expressive of or showing disbelief: *an incredulous stare.* **3.** USAGE PROBLEM Hard or impossible to believe.

[From Latin *incrēdulus* : *in-*, not + *crēdulus,* believing.]

RELATED WORDS:

adverb—**in·cred′u·lous·ly**
noun—**in·cred′u·lous·ness**

SEE NOTE AT **incredible** (# 45).

"I felt the floe I stood on begin to shake, then wobble, and before me the ice parted to reveal the cold, muddy swirl twisting below—a more fearsome thing I'd never seen. The frozen river wasn't locked in place as I'd supposed but was being forced slowly downstream, buckling, snapping, opening, closing, ready to swallow whatever came onto it. That's when common sense and terror hit and I headed for shore, unsure whether to go gently and slowly or hard and fast. . . . When I reached land, I looked back, incredulous that I'd thought I could actually make it across."

—William Least Heat-Moon,
River-Horse

47

in·fer (ĭn-fûr′)

transitive verb

Past participle and past tense: **in·ferred**
Present participle: **in·fer·ring**
Third person singular present tense: **in·fers**

1. To conclude from evidence or reasoning: *"Unlike many other functions, reading cannot be studied in animals; indeed, for many years the cerebral localization of all higher cognitive processes could be inferred only from the effects of brain injuries on the people who survived them"* (Sally E. Shaywitz, *Scientific American*). **2.** To hint; imply.

[Latin *īnferre,* to bring in, adduce : *in-*, in + *ferre,* to bear.]

RELATED WORDS:

adjective—**in·fer′a·ble**
adverb—**in·fer′a·bly**
noun—**in′fer·ence**

Infer is sometimes confused with *imply,* but it makes good sense to keep these verbs distinct. Inference is the activity performed by a reader or interpreter in drawing conclusions that are not explicit in what is said: *When the mayor said that she would not rule out a tax increase, we inferred that she had been consulting with some new financial advisers, since her old advisers were in favor of tax reductions.* On the other hand, when we say that a speaker or sentence implies something, we mean that it is conveyed or suggested without being stated outright: *When the mayor said that she would not rule out a business tax increase, she implied* (not *inferred*) *that some taxes might be raised.*

48

in·flam·ma·ble (ĭn-flăm′ə-bəl)

adjective

Easily ignited and capable of burning rapidly; flammable: "*Slurry decomposes in storage and produces a mixture of gases. . . . All are unpleasant, some can be inflammable, and one in particular, hydrogen sulphide, is extremely poisonous to humans and animals alike*" (Edna O'Brien, *Wild Decembers*).

[Middle English, liable to inflammation, from Medieval Latin *īnflammābilis,* from Latin *īnflammāre.*]

RELATED WORDS:

noun—**in·flam′ma·bil′i·ty**
noun—**in·flam′ma·ble**
adverb—**in·flam′ma·bly**

Historically, *flammable* and *inflammable* mean the same thing. However, the presence of the prefix *in–* has misled many people into assuming that *inflammable* means "not flammable" or "noncombustible." The prefix *in–* in *inflammable* is not, however, the Latin negative prefix *in–*, which is related to the English *un–* and appears in such words as *indecent* and *inglorious.* Rather, this *in–* is an intensive prefix derived from the Latin preposition *in.* This prefix also appears in the word *inflame.* But many people are not aware of this derivation, and for clarity's sake it is advisable to use only *flammable* if you want to give a warning. If you wish to refer to the inability to catch on fire, use *nonflammable*, which is unambiguous.

49

in·sure (ĭn-sho͝or′)

transitive verb

Past participle and past tense: **in·sured**
Present participle: **in·sur·ing**
Third person singular present tense: **in·sures**

1a. To provide or arrange insurance for: *"In the past two years, the number of patients [who are] insured by managed care plans has grown by about one-third"* (Lisa Belkin, *New York Times Magazine*). **b.** To acquire or have insurance for: *"More than 300,000 laptops were stolen last year alone, and so the company insures each bag with a computer compartment for up to $1,500 if it's stolen in the first year"* (Stephanie Cook, *Christian Science Monitor*). **2.** To make sure, certain, or secure: *"By relying primarily on voluntary cooperation and private enterprise . . . we can insure that the private sector is a check on the powers of the governmental sector and an effective protection of freedom of speech, of religion, and of thought"* (Milton Friedman, *Capitalism and Freedom*).

[Middle English *ensuren,* to assure, from Old French *enseurer,* possibly variant of *assurer.*]

RELATED WORDS:

noun—**in·sur′a·bil′i·ty**
adjective—**in·sur′a·ble**

Assure, ensure, and *insure* all mean "to make secure or certain." Only *assure* is used with reference to a person in the sense of "to set the mind at rest": *The ambassador assured the Prime Minister of his loyalty.* Although *ensure* and *insure* are generally interchangeable, only *insure* is now widely used in American English in the commercial sense of "to guarantee persons or property against risk."

50

i·ro·ny (ī′rə-nē, ī′ər-nē)

noun

Plural: **i·ro·nies**

1a. The use of words to express something different from and often opposite to their literal meaning. **b.** An expression or utterance marked by a deliberate contrast between apparent and intended meaning. **c.** A literary style employing such contrasts for humorous or rhetorical effect. **2a.** Incongruity between what might be expected and what actually occurs. **b.** An occurrence, result, or circumstance notable for such incongruity. **3.** The dramatic effect achieved by leading an audience to understand an incongruity between a situation in a play and its accompanying speeches, while the characters remain unaware of the incongruity; dramatic irony.

[French *ironie*, from Old French, from Latin *īrōnīa*, from Greek *eirōneia*, feigned ignorance, from *eirōn*, dissembler, probably from *eirein*, to say.]

RELATED WORDS:

adjective—**i·ron′ic**
adverb—**i·ron′i·cal·ly**

The words *ironic, irony,* and *ironically* are sometimes used of events and circumstances that might better be described as simply "coincidental" or "improbable," in that they suggest no particular lessons about human vanity or folly. The Usage Panel dislikes the looser use of these words; 78 percent rejected the use of *ironically* in the sentence *In 1969 Susie moved from Ithaca to California where she met her husband-to-be, who, ironically, also came from upstate New York.* Some Panelists noted that this particular usage might be acceptable if Susie had in fact moved to California in order to find a husband, in which case the story could be taken as exemplifying the folly of supposing that we can know what fate has in store for us. By contrast, 73 percent accepted the sentence *Ironically, even as the government was fulminating against American policy, American jeans and videocassettes were the hottest items in the stalls of the market,* where the incongruity of the government's statements and the practices it tolerates as necessary can be seen as an example of human inconsistency.

51

ir·re·gard·less (ĭr′ĭ-gärd′lĭs)

adverb

NONSTANDARD Regardless.

[Probably blend of *irrespective* and *regardless.*]

Irregardless is a word that many mistakenly believe to be correct usage in formal style, when in fact it is used chiefly in nonstandard speech or casual writing. Coined in the United States in the early 20th century, it has met with a blizzard of condemnation for being an improper yoking of *irrespective* and *regardless* and for the logical absurdity of combining the negative *ir–* prefix and *–less* suffix in a single term. Although one might reasonably argue that it is no different from words with redundant affixes like *debone* and *unravel,* it has been considered a blunder for decades and will probably continue to be so.

52

its (ĭts)

adjective

The possessive form of **it.** Used as a modifier before a noun: *The airline canceled its early flight to New York.*

[Alteration of *it's* : *it* + 's.]

SEE NOTE AT **it's** (# 53).

it's (ĭts)

1. Contraction of *it is.* **2.** Contraction of *it has.*

Its is the possessive form of the pronoun *it* and is correctly written without an apostrophe: *The kitten licked its paws.* It should not be confused with the contraction *it's* (for *it is* or *it has*), which should always have an apostrophe: *It's snowing outside. It's been years since I've visited Chicago.*

54

ku·dos (ko͞o′dōz′, ko͞o′dōs′, ko͞o′dŏs′, kyo͞o′dōz′, kyo͞o′dōs′, kyo͞o′dŏs′)

noun

Acclaim or praise for exceptional achievement.

[Greek *kūdos,* magical glory.]

Kudos is one of those words like *congeries* that look like plurals but are etymologically singular. Acknowledging the Greek history of the term requires *Kudos is* (not *are*) *due her for her brilliant work on the score.* But *kudos* has often been treated as a plural, especially in the popular press, as in *She received many kudos for her work.* This plural use has given rise to the singular form *kudo.* These innovations follow the pattern whereby the English words *pea* and *cherry* were shortened from nouns ending in an (s) sound (English *pease* and French *cerise*), that were mistakenly thought to be plural. The singular *kudo* remains far less common than the plural use; both are often viewed as incorrect in more formal contexts.

It is worth noting that even people who are careful to treat *kudos* only as a singular often pronounce it as if it were a plural. Etymology would require that the final consonant be pronounced as a voiceless (s), as we do in *pathos,* another word derived from Greek, rather than as a voiced (z).

55

lay (lā)

verb

Past participle and past tense: **laid**
Present participle: **lay·ing**
Third person singular present tense: **lays**

transitive **1a.** To place or put, especially on a flat surface or in a horizontal position: *I laid the baby in the crib.* **b.** To put or place in a certain position or condition: *The remark laid him open to criticism.* **2.** To put in place; set down: *The workers are laying tiles down in the kitchen.* **3.** To produce (an egg or eggs). **4.** To cause to subside or become calm: "*. . . chas'd the clouds, and laid the winds*" (John Milton, *Paradise Regained*). **5.** To put in order; prepare: "*He did not look at her but busied himself with his breakfast. . . He prepared coffee and laid the table*" (Carson McCullers, *The Heart Is a Lonely Hunter*). **6.** To spread over a surface: *The artist lays paint on the canvas.* **7.** To impose as a burden or punishment: *The police officer laid a fine on the offender.* **8.** To put forth; present for examination: *The lawyer laid the case before the court.* **9.** To place or give (importance, for example): *The teacher lays great value on correct grammar.* **10.** To assign; charge: *They laid the blame on us.* **11.** To place (a bet); wager: *At the race track, the gambler laid $100 on his favorite horse.*

intransitive To produce an egg or eggs: *The hens stopped laying suddenly.*

noun

The way in which something is situated or organized: *"Duane peered through the branches and studied the lay of the land"* (Zane Grey, *The Lone Star Ranger*).

[Middle English *leien,* from Old English *lecgan.*]

✎ *Lay* ("to put, place, or prepare") and *lie* ("to recline or be situated") have been confused for centuries; evidence exists that *lay* has been used to mean "lie" since the 1300s. Why? First, there are two *lays*. One is the base form of the verb *lay,* and the other is the past tense of *lie.* Second, *lay* was once used with a reflexive pronoun to mean "lie" and survives in the familiar line from the child's prayer *Now I lay me down to sleep; lay me down* is easily shortened to *lay down.* Third, *lay down,* as in *She lay down on the sofa* sounds the same as *laid down,* as in *I laid down the law to the kids.* It's not surprising that all this similarity of sound has produced confusion of usage, but traditional grammar requires that the two words be kept distinct.

Lay and *lie* are most easily distinguished by the following guidelines: *Lay* is a transitive verb and takes a direct object. *Lay* and its principal parts (*laid, laying*) are correctly used in the following examples: *He laid* (not *lay*) *the newspaper on the table. The table was laid for four. Lie* is an intransitive verb and cannot take an object. *Lie* and its principal parts (*lay, lain, lying*) are correctly used in the following examples: *She often lies* (not *lays*) *down after lunch. When I lay* (not *laid*) *down, I fell asleep. The garbage had lain* (not *laid*) *there a week. I was lying* (not *laying*) *in bed when he called.*

56

leave (lēv)

verb

Past participle and past tense: **left**
Present participle: **leav·ing**
Third person singular present tense: **leaves**

transitive

1. To go out of or go away from: *After she finished the report, she left the office.* **2.** To end one's association with; withdraw from: *After ten years in the service, he left the navy for civilian life.* **3.** To go without taking or removing; forget: *I left my book on the bus.* **4.** To allow to remain unused: *I left some milk in the glass.* **5.** To allow to remain in a certain condition or place: *He left the lights on all night.* **6.** To give to another to control, act on, or use; entrust: *Leave all the details to us.* **7.** To give by will; bequeath: *"Jonah argued that men liked to make a surprise of their wills, while Martha said that nobody need be surprised if he left the best part of his money to those who least expected it"* (George Eliot, *Middlemarch*). **8.** To have as a result, consequence, or remainder: *The car left a trail of exhaust fumes. Two from eight leaves six.* **9.** NONSTANDARD To allow or permit; let.

intransitive To set out or depart; go: *We left after lunch.*

IDIOM:

leave alone *or* **let alone** To refrain from disturbing or interfering with: "*'Leave my books alone!' he said. 'You might have thrown them aside if you had liked, but as to soiling them like that, it is disgusting!'*" (Thomas Hardy, *Jude the Obscure*).

[Middle English *leaven*, from Old English *lǣfan*.]

In formal writing, *leave* is not an acceptable substitute for *let* in the sense "to allow or permit." Thus in the following examples, only *let* can be used: *Let me be. Let him go. Let it lie.*

Leave alone is an acceptable substitute for *let alone* in the sense "to refrain from disturbing or interfering with," as in *Left alone, he was quite productive.* However, there are some who do not accept this usage and feel that *leave alone* should mean simply "to depart from someone who remains in solitude," as in *They were left alone in the wilderness.*

less (lĕs)

adjective

A comparative of **little. 1.** Not as great in amount or quantity: *I have less money than I did yesterday.* **2.** Lower in importance, esteem, or rank: *The speaker was no less a person than the ambassador.* **3.** Consisting of a smaller number.

preposition

With the deduction of; minus: *Five less two is three.*

adverb

The comparative of **little.** To a smaller extent, degree, or frequency: "*We replaced and screwed down the lid, and, having secured the door of iron, made our way, with toil, into the scarcely less gloomy apartments of the upper portion of the house*" (Edgar Allan Poe, *The Fall of the House of Usher*).

noun

1. A smaller amount: *She received less than she asked for.* **2.** Something not as important as something else: *People have been punished for less.*

IDIOMS:

less than Not at all: *He had a less than favorable view of the matter.*

much less *or* **still less** Certainly not: *I'm not blaming anyone, much less you.*

[Middle English *lesse,* from Old English *lǣssa* (*adjective*), and *lǣs* (*adverb*).]

SEE NOTE AT **fewer** (# 34).

let (lĕt)

verb

Past participle and past tense: **let**
Present participle: **let·ting**
Third person singular present tense: **lets**

1. To give permission or opportunity to; allow: *I let them borrow the car. The inheritance money let us finally buy a house.* **2.** To cause to; make: *Let me know what happens.* **3.** Used as an auxiliary verb to express a command, request, or warning: *Let's finish the job!* **4.** Used as an auxiliary verb to express a proposal or assumption: *Let x equal 3.* **5.** To permit to enter, proceed, or depart: *"When we returned home, we let the dogs out, as we always did, to run around before they were shut in for the night"* (Lydia Davis, *St. Martin*). **6.** To permit escape; release: *Who let the air out of the balloon?* **7.** To rent or lease: *The landlord lets rooms to students.*

intransitive To become rented or leased: *The apartment lets for $900 a month.*

IDIOMS:

let alone **1.** Not to mention; much less: *"Their ancestors had been dirt poor and never saw royalty, let alone hung around with them"* (Garrison Keillor, *Lake Wobegon Days*). **2.** *or* **leave alone** To refrain from disturbing or interfering: *"'Let me alone! let me alone!' sobbed Catherine. 'If I've done wrong, I'm dying for it. It is enough!'"* (Emily Brontë, *Wuthering Heights*).

let go To cease to employ; dismiss: *The factory let 20 workers go.*

[Middle English *leten,* from Old English *lǣtan.*]

SEE NOTE AT **leave** (# 56).

lie (lī)

intransitive verb

Past tense: **lay**
Past participle: **lain**
Present participle: **ly·ing**
Third person singular present tense: **lies**

1. To place oneself at rest in a flat, horizontal, or resting position; recline: *He lay under a tree to sleep.* **2.** To be in a flat, horizontal, or resting position: *"I collected the instruments of life around me, that I might infuse a spark of being into the lifeless thing that lay at my feet"* (Mary Wollstonecraft Shelley, *Frankenstein*). **3.** To be or rest on a surface: *Dirty dishes lay on the table.* **4.** To be located: *The lake lies beyond this hill.* **5.** To remain in a certain position or condition: *The dust has lain undisturbed for years.* **6.** To consist or have as a basis: *"Eric was pleased, but he always reminded himself that his success lay in promoting the talent of others"* (Louis Auchincloss, *Her Infinite Variety*). **7.** To extend: *Our land lies between these trees and the river.* **8.** To be buried in a specified place: *His ancestors lie in the town cemetery.*

noun

The manner or position in which something is situated, as the surface or slope of a piece of land.

[Middle English *lien,* from Old English *licgan.*]

SEE NOTE AT **lay** (# 55).

"It was on a dreary night of November that I beheld the accomplishment of my toils. With an anxiety that almost amounted to agony, I collected the instruments of life around me, that I might infuse a spark of being into the lifeless thing that lay at my feet. It was already one in the morning; the rain pattered dismally against the panes, and my candle was nearly burnt out, when, by the glimmer of the half-extinguished light, I saw the dull yellow eye of the creature open; it breathed hard, and a convulsive motion agitated its limbs."

— Mary Wollstonecraft Shelley,
Frankenstein

lit·er·al·ly (lĭt′ər-ə-lē)

adverb

1. In a literal manner; word for word: *The scholar translated the Greek passage literally.* **2.** In a literal or strict sense: *Don't take my remarks literally.* **3.** USAGE PROBLEM Really; actually. Used as an intensive before a figurative expression: *He was laughing so hard his sides literally burst.*

For more than a hundred years, critics have remarked on the incoherence of using *literally* in a way that suggests the exact opposite of its primary sense of "in a manner that accords with the literal sense of the words." In 1926, for example, H.W. Fowler deplored the example *"The 300,000 Unionists . . . will be literally thrown to the wolves."* The practice reflects a tendency to use certain adverbs, like *completely* and *unbelievably,* as general intensifiers, without calling to mind the primary sense of the adjective from which the adverb is made. In this regard, *literally* is very similar to the adverb *really,* whose intensive use often has nothing to do with what is "real," as in *They really dropped the ball in marketing that product.*

With regard to *literally,* the Usage Panel supports the traditional view. In our 2004 survey, only 23 percent of the Panel accepted the following sentence, in which *literally* undercuts the sentence's central metaphor: *The situation was especially grim in England where industrialism was literally swallowing the country's youth.* The Panel mustered more enthusiasm for the use of *literally* with a dead metaphor, which functions as a set phrase and evokes no image for most people. Some 37 percent accepted *He was literally out of his mind with worry.* But when there is no metaphor at all, a substantial majority of the Panel was willing to allow *literally* to be used as an intensifier; 66 percent accepted the sentence *They had literally no help from the government on the project.*

mass (măs)

noun

1. A measure of the amount of matter contained in or constituting a physical body: "*The Sun will swallow the planet Mercury and its outer rim will reach beyond the present orbit of Venus. Our sister planet will no longer be there, however, because as the Sun has lost mass, its gravitational pull on Venus (and Earth) has become less, and these planets have moved away from the encroaching fires*" (James Trefil, *Smithsonian*). **2.** A unified body of matter with no specific shape: "*Cooks throughout the many nations also use yams, cassavas, green bananas and plantains. These staples are tasty on their own or combined with other ingredients to make a starchy mass for scooping up savory dishes*" (Jonell Nash, *Essence*). **3.** A large but nonspecific amount or number: *A mass of people entered the stadium.* **4.** The principal part; the majority: *The mass of the continent was visible from the rocketship.* **5.** The physical bulk or size of a solid body: *The huge mass of the ocean liner crept into the harbor.* **6. masses** The body of common people or people of low socioeconomic status: "*Give me your tired, your poor, / Your huddled masses yearning to breathe free*" (Emma Lazarus, *The New Colossus*).

verb

Past participle and past tense: **massed**
Present participle: **mass·ing**
Third person singular present tense: **mass·es**

transitive To gather into a mass: "*[T]he population massed itself and moved toward the river, met the children coming in an open carriage drawn by shouting citizens, thronged around it, joined its homeward march, and swept magnificently up the main street roaring huzzah after huzzah!*" (Mark Twain, *The Adventures of Tom Sawyer*).

intransitive To be gathered into a mass: *The hikers massed together to stay warm.*

adjective

1. Of, relating to, characteristic of, directed at, or attended by a large number of people: *mass communication.* **2.** Done or carried out on a large scale: *mass production.* **3.** Total; complete: *The mass result is impressive.*

[Middle English *masse,* from Old French, from Latin *massa,* from Greek *māza, maza.*]

✍ Although most hand-held calculators can translate pounds into kilograms, an absolute conversion factor between these two units is not technically sound. A pound is a unit of force, and a kilogram is a unit of mass. When the unit pound is used to indicate the force that a gravitational field exerts on a mass, the pound is a unit of weight. Mistaking weight for mass is tantamount to confusing the electric charges on two objects with the forces of attraction (or repulsion) between them. Like charge, the mass of an object is an intrinsic property of that object: electrons have a unique mass, protons have a unique mass, and some particles, such as photons, have no mass. Weight, on the other hand, is a force due to the gravitational attraction between two bodies. For example, one's weight on the Moon is ⅙ of one's weight on Earth. Nevertheless, one's mass on the Moon is identical to one's mass on Earth. The reason that hand-held calculators can translate between units of weight and units of mass is that the majority of us use calculators on the planet Earth at or near sea level, where the conversion factor is constant for all practical purposes.

mean (mēn)

noun

1. Something having a position, quality, or condition midway between extremes; a medium. **2.** A number that typifies a set of numbers, especially an arithmetic mean or average. **3.** Either the second or third term of a proportion of four terms. In the proportion ⅔ = 4/6, the means are 3 and 4. **4. means** *(used with a singular or plural verb)* A method, a course of action, or an instrument by which an act can be accomplished or an end achieved: *The solar panels provide a practical means of using the sun's energy to generate electricity.* **5. means** *(used with a plural verb)* Money, property, or other wealth: *The mayor was a person of means and bankrolled his election campaign.*

adjective

1. Occupying a middle or intermediate position between two extremes: *The school district analyzed the mean test scores of each class.* **2.** Intermediate in size, extent, quality, time, or degree; average.

IDIOMS:

by any means In any way possible: *We must fix this problem by any means.*

by no means In no sense; certainly not: *By no means should you go sailing in rough weather.*

[Middle English *mene,* middle, from Old French *meien,* from Latin *mediānus,* from *medius.*]

In the sense of "financial resources" *means* takes a plural verb: *His means are more than adequate.* In the sense of "a way to an end," *means* may be treated as either a singular or plural. It is singular when referring to a particular strategy or method: *The best means of securing the cooperation of the builders is to appeal to their self-interest.* It is plural when it refers to a group of strategies or methods: *The most effective means for dealing with the drug problem have generally been those suggested by the affected communities.*

Means is most often followed by *of*: *a means of noise reduction.* But *for, to,* and *toward* are also used: *a means for transmitting sound; a means to an end; a means toward achieving equality.*

63

me·di·an (mē′dē-ən)

noun

1. Something that lies halfway between two extremes; a medium. **2.** The middle number of a sequence having an odd number of values or the average of the two middle values if the sequence has an even number of values. For example, in the sequence 1, 2, 5, 10, 19, the median is 5; in the sequence 7, 8, 12, 16, the median is 10. **3a.** A line that joins a vertex of a triangle to the midpoint of the opposite side. **b.** The line that joins the midpoints of the nonparallel sides of a trapezoid.

adjective

1. Located in or extending toward the middle: *The lanes of traffic were separated by a median barrier.* **2.** Constituting the middle value in a set of numbers: *The statisticians analyzed the median score.*

[Latin *mediānus,* from *medius,* middle.]

In statistics, the concepts of *average* and *median* are often confused. To calculate an average, you add up all the items under consideration, and then divide by the number of items. So, for example, if a real estate agent sells five houses worth $95,000, $115,000, $190,000, $260,000, and $800,000, the average sales price is $292,000. Determining the *median* involves looking at the middle value in a series of values (if the series contains an even number of values, you then take the average of the middle two values). Using the above prices, the median sales price of these homes was $190,000. Median prices are often reported because it tells you that the same number of items fall above that value as fall below it, whereas if one of the values is much greater or lower than the other values, reporting the average may seem skewed, as in the example above.

64 **mis·chie·vous** (mĭs′chə-vəs)

adjective

1. Causing mischief; naughty: *"I've left my young children to look after themselves, and a more mischievous and troublesome set of young imps doesn't exist, ma'am"* (Kenneth Grahame, *The Wind in the Willows*). **2.** Showing a tendency or intent to play pranks or tease: *The child cast a mischievous glance.* **3.** Causing injury or damage: *The hard drive was destroyed by a mischievous computer virus.*

[Middle English *mischevous,* from *mischef,* mischief, from Old French *meschief,* misfortune, from *meschever,* to end badly : *mes-,* badly + *chever,* to happen, come to an end (from Vulgar Latin **capāre,* to come to a head, from **capum,* head, from Latin *caput*).]

RELATED WORDS:

adverb—**mis′chie·vous·ly**
noun—**mis′chie·vous·ness**

The pronunciation (mĭs-chē′vē-əs) is considered nonstandard, and is an example of *intrusion,* a phonological process that involves the addition or insertion of an extra sound. *Mischievous* is properly pronounced with three syllables, with the accent on the first syllable. The word is often misspelled with the suffix *-ious,* which matches the mispronunciation.

65

nu·cle·ar (no͞o′klē-ər, nyo͞o′klē-ər)

adjective

1. Of, relating to, or forming a nucleus: *The biologist studied the cell's nuclear membrane under a microscope.* **2.** Of or relating to atomic nuclei: *"December 2 [1942]: Scientists at the University of Chicago achieve the first sustained nuclear chain reaction in human history"* (Alan Brinkley & Davis Dyer, eds., *The Reader's Companion to the American Presidency*). **3.** Using or derived from the energy of atomic nuclei: *"[A]n attack on a nuclear power plant would not automatically mean a disaster on the scale of Chernobyl"* (Sonya Yee, *Christian Science Monitor).* **4.** Relating to, having, or involving atomic or hydrogen bombs: *"In the early 1980s, the U.S. experienced a nuclear hysteria—a morbid, near panicked fear of nuclear apocalypse"* (Charles Krauthammer, *Time*).

[Adjectival form of *nucleus,* from Latin *nuculeus,* nucleus, kernel, from *nucula,* little nut, diminutive of *nux, nuc-,* nut.]

The pronunciation (no͞o′kyə-lər), which is generally considered incorrect, is an example of how a familiar phonological pattern can influence an unfamiliar one. The usual pronunciation of the final two syllables of this word is (-klē-ər), but this sequence of sounds is rare in English. Much more common is the similar sequence (-kyə-lər), which occurs in words like *particular, circular, spectacular,* and in many scientific words like *molecular, ocular*, and *vascular*. Adjusted to fit into this familiar pattern, the (-kyə-lər) pronunciation is often heard in high places. It is not uncommon in the military, even among commanders, in association with nuclear weaponry, and it has been a notable characteristic of the speech of presidents Dwight Eisenhower, Jimmy Carter, and George W. Bush. The prominence of these speakers, however, has done little to brighten the appeal of (no͞o′kyə-lər) for many others.

66

pa·ram·e·ter (pə-răm′ĭ-tər)

noun

1. A variable or an arbitrary constant appearing in a mathematical expression, each value of which restricts or determines the specific form of the expression. **2a.** One of a set of measurable factors, such as temperature and pressure, that define a system and determine its behavior and are varied in an experiment. **b.** USAGE PROBLEM A factor that restricts what is possible or what results. **c.** A factor that determines a range of variations; a boundary: *The principal of the experimental school made sure that the parameters of its curriculum continued to expand.* **3.** USAGE PROBLEM A distinguishing characteristic or feature.

[New Latin *parametrum*, a line through the focus and parallel to the directrix of a conic : Greek *para-*, beside + Greek *metron*, measure.]

RELATED WORDS:

verb—**pa·ram′e·ter·ize′** (pə-răm′ə-tə-rīz′)
adjective—**par′a·met′ric** (păr′ə-mĕt′rĭk)
adverb—**par′a·met′ri·cal·ly**

🙞 The term *parameter,* which originates in mathematics, has a number of specific meanings in fields such as astronomy, electricity, crystallography, and statistics. Perhaps because of its ring of technical authority, people have applied *parameter* more generally in recent years to refer to any factor that determines a range of variations and especially to a factor that restricts what results from a process or policy. In this use, the word *parameter* is used to mean "the particular value of a parameter," and comes close to meaning "a set limit or boundary." For example, a budget can be thought of as a set of parameters that determine a range of activity, much like a set of mathematical parameters that establish the range of effects, or limits, of other variables. The sentence *A budget is a framework that defines the financial parameters within which an organization operates* was considered acceptable by 81 percent of the Usage Panel in our 2004 survey. *Parameter* is sometimes used incorrectly when it does not denote a range of variation, as if it were a technical-sounding synonym for *characteristic.* In 1988, 88 percent of the Usage Panel rejected the sentence *The Judeo-Christian ethic is one of the important parameters of Western culture.* In 2004, 77 percent rejected this same sentence, suggesting that familiarity has not bred tolerance of this usage.

67

pe·nul·ti·mate (pĭ-nŭl′tə-mĭt)

adjective

1. Next to last: *"His cause for beatification, the penultimate step before sainthood, is still on course"* (Alessandra Stanley, *New York Times*). **2.** Of or relating to the next-to-last syllable of a word: *The word* renewal *has penultimate stress.*

noun

The next to the last.

[From Latin *paenultimus,* next to last : *paene,* almost + *ultimus,* last.]

RELATED WORD:

adverb—**pe·nul′ti·mate·ly**

Penultimate is sometimes mistakenly used where the word *ultimate* is called for, especially in the sense of "representing or exhibiting the greatest possible development or sophistication" as in the sentence *This car is the penultimate in engineering design.* This mistake is probably due to a misconception that *pen-* is a prefix that acts as an intensifier of the word *ultimate,* when it actually derives from the Latin word *paene,* meaning "almost." Thus, people who know the correct meaning of *penultimate* would reject its use as a synonym of *ultimate* and they may view the speaker or writer as not only pretentious, but ignorant as well.

68

per·suade (pər-swād′)

transitive verb

Past participle and past tense: **per·suad·ed**
Present participle: **per·suad·ing**
Third person singular present tense: **per·suades**

To cause (someone) to do or believe something by means of argument, reasoning, or entreaty: *"Lord cardinal, will your grace / Persuade the queen to send the Duke of York / Unto his princely brother presently?"* (William Shakespeare, *Richard III*).

[Latin *persuādēre* : *per-*, per- + *suādēre,* to urge.]

RELATED WORD:

adjective—**per·suad′a·ble**
noun—**per·suad′er**

SEE NOTE AT **convince** (# 22).

"Fie, what an indirect and peevish course
Is this of hers! Lord cardinal, will your grace
Persuade the queen to send the Duke of York
Unto his princely brother presently?
If she deny, Lord Hastings, go with him,
And from her jealous arms pluck him perforce."

—William Shakespeare,
Richard III

69

pe·ruse (pə-ro͞oz′)

transitive verb

Past participle and past tense: **pe·rused**
Present participle: **pe·rus·ing**
Third person singular present tense: **pe·rus·es**

To read or examine, typically with great care: *"He that shall peruse the political pamphlets of any past reign, will wonder why they were so eagerly read, or so loudly praised"* (Samuel Johnson, *The Rambler*).

[Middle English *perusen,* to use up : Latin *per-,* per- + Middle English *usen,* to use.]

RELATED WORDS:

adjective—**pe·rus′a·ble**
noun—**pe·rus′al**
noun—**pe·rus′er**

Peruse has long meant "to read thoroughly," as in *He perused the contract until he was satisfied that it met all of his requirements,* which was acceptable to 75 percent of the Usage Panel in our 2011 survey. But the word is often used more loosely, to mean simply "to read," as in *The librarians checked to see which titles had been perused in the last month and which ones had been left untouched.* Seventy percent of the Panel rejected this example in 1999, but only 39 percent rejected it in 2011. Further extension of the word to mean "to glance over, skim" has traditionally been considered an error, but our ballot results suggest that it is becoming somewhat more acceptable. When asked about the sentence *I only had a moment to peruse the manual quickly,* 66 percent of the Panel found it unacceptable in 1988, 58 percent in 1999, and 48 percent in 2011. Use of the word outside of reading contexts, as in *We perused the shops in the downtown area,* is often considered a mistake.

70

phe·nom·e·non (fə-nŏm′ə-nŏn)

noun

1. (Plural: **phe·nom·e·na**) An occurrence, circumstance, or fact that is perceptible by the senses or with aid of instrumentation: *"Typical manifestations of T cells at work include such diverse phenomena as the rejection of a foreign skin graft and the killing of tumor cells"* (Gary W. Litman, *Scientific American*). **2.** (Plural: **phe·nom·e·nons**) A remarkable, significant, or outstanding person or thing: *"In an industry famous for cutthroat competition, this summer's reality TV shows have become a pop culture phenomenon and left a string of stunned TV executives scrambling to catch up"* (Lauren Hunter, *cnn.com*).

[Late Latin *phaenomenon,* from Greek *phainomenon,* from neuter present participle of *phainesthai,* to appear.]

The word *phenomenon* comes to us from Greek via Latin and usually keeps its Greek plural form *phenomena* when it means "an occurrence, circumstance, or fact that is perceptible by the senses." You may sometimes come across *phenomena* used as a singular noun, as in *This is a very strange phenomena,* but this usage is widely considered incorrect. The plural *phenomenons* is used frequently in nonscientific writing when the meaning is "extraordinary things, occurrences, or persons," as in *The Beatles were phenomenons in the history of rock 'n' roll.*

plus (plŭs)

conjunction

1. Added to: *Three plus two equals five.* **2.** Increased by; along with: *Their strength plus their spirit makes them formidable.* **3.** USAGE PROBLEM And: *I bought a dining table, plus four chairs and a mirror.*

adjective

1. Positive or on the positive part of a scale: *a temperature of plus five degrees.* **2.** Added or extra: *a plus benefit.* **3.** *Informal* Increased to a further degree or number: *"At 70 plus, [he] is old enough to be metaphysical"* (Anatole Broyard, *New York Times Book Review*). **4.** Ranking on the higher end of a designated scale: *I received a grade of B plus in chemistry.* **5.** Relating to or designating an electric charge of a sign opposite to that of an electron; positive.

noun

Plural **plus·es** *or* **plus·ses**

1. The plus sign (+). **2.** A positive quantity. **3.** A favorable condition or factor: *The clear weather was a plus for the golf tournament.*

[Latin *plūs*, more.]

❧ When mathematical equations are pronounced as English sentences, the verb is usually in the singular: *Two plus two* is (or *equals*) *four.* By the same token, subjects containing two noun phrases joined by *plus* are usually construed as singular: *The construction slowdown plus the bad weather has made for a weak market.* This observation has led some to argue that in these sentences, *plus* functions as a preposition meaning "in addition to." But if this were true, the *plus* phrase could be moved to the beginning of the sentence. Clearly, this is not the case—we do not say *Plus the bad weather, the construction slowdown has made for a weak market.* It makes more sense to view *plus* in these uses as a conjunction that joins two subjects into a single entity requiring a single verb by notional agreement, just as *and* does in the sentence *Chips and beans* is *her favorite appetizer.*

The use of *plus* introducing an independent clause has long been considered infelicitous, if not wrong. But a clear majority of the Usage Panel accepts it. In our 2009 survey, 67 percent accepted the example *He has a lot of personal charm. Plus, he knows what he's doing.* Some 63 percent accepted an example expressing negative judgment: *We were a terrible team. Plus, we had bad uniforms.*

72

pre·cip·i·tate (prĭ-sĭpʹĭ-tātʹ)

verb

Past participle and past tense: **pre·cip·i·tat·ed**
Present participle: **pre·cip·i·tat·ing**
Third person singular present tense: **pre·cip·i·tates**

transitive **1.** To throw from or as if from a great height; hurl downward: *"[T]he finest bridge in all Peru broke and precipitated five travelers into the gulf below"* (Thornton Wilder, *The Bridge of San Luis Rey*). **2.** To cause to happen, especially suddenly or prematurely: *The political scandal precipitated a torrent of legislative reforms.* **3.** To cause (water vapor) to condense and fall from the air as rain, snow, sleet, or hail. **4.** To cause (a solid substance) to be separated from a solution: *The chemist precipitated the minerals from the water by adding borax.*

intransitive **1.** To condense and fall from the air as rain, snow, sleet, or hail. **2.** To be separated from a solution as a solid.

adjective (prĭ-sĭp′ĭ-tĭt)

1. Moving rapidly and heedlessly; speeding headlong: *The meteorologists tracked the tornado's precipitate course.* **2.** Acting with or marked by excessive haste and lack of due deliberation; reckless: *They soon came to regret the precipitate decisions.* **3.** Occurring suddenly or unexpectedly: *The pundits couldn't explain the precipitate rise in oil prices.*

noun (prĭ-sĭp′ĭ-tāt′, prĭ-sĭp′ĭ-tĭt)

A chemical solid or solid phase separated from a solution.

[Latin *praecipitāre, praecipitāt-*, to throw headlong, from *praeceps, praecipit-*, headlong : *prae-*, pre- + *caput, capit-*, head.]

RELATED WORDS:

adverb—**pre·cip′i·tate·ly**
adjective—**pre·cip′i·ta′tive**
noun—**pre·cip′i·ta′tor**

SEE NOTE AT **precipitous** (# 73).

73

pre·cip·i·tous (prĭ-sĭp′ĭ-təs)

adjective

1. Resembling a precipice; extremely steep. **2.** Having several precipices: "*The Duchy of Grand Fenwick lies in a precipitous fold of the northern Alps and embraces in its tumbling landscape portions of three valleys, a river, one complete mountain with an elevation of two thousand feet and a castle*" (Leonard Wibberley, *The Mouse That Roared*). **3.** USAGE PROBLEM Extremely rapid, hasty, or abrupt; precipitate.

[Probably from obsolete *precipitious,* from Latin *praecipitium,* precipice.]

RELATED WORDS:

adverb—**pre·cip′i·tous·ly**
noun—**pre·cip′i·tous·ness**

The adjective *precipitate* and the adverb *precipitately* were once applied to physical steepness but are now used primarily of rash, headlong actions: *Precipitous* currently means "steep" in both literal and figurative senses: *the precipitous rapids of the upper river; a precipitous drop in commodity prices.* But *precipitous* and *precipitously* are also frequently used to mean "abrupt, hasty," which takes them into territory that would ordinarily belong to *precipitate* and *precipitately: their precipitous decision to leave.* This usage is a natural extension of the use of *precipitous* to describe a rise or fall in a quantity over time: *a precipitous increase in reports of measles* is also an abrupt or sudden event. Although the extended use of *precipitous* is well attested in the work of reputable writers, it is still widely regarded as an error and was considered unacceptable to two-thirds of the Usage Panel in 2001.

74

pre·scribe (prĭ-skrīb′)

verb

Past participle and past tense: **pre·scribed**
Present participle: **pre·scrib·ing**
Third person singular present tense: **pre·scribes**

transitive **1.** To set down as a rule or guide; impose or direct: *"In all well-governed states too, not only judges are appointed for determining the controversies of individuals, but rules are prescribed for regulating the decisions of those judges"* (Adam Smith, *The Theory of Moral Sentiments*). **2.** To order the use of (a medicine or other treatment): *The doctor prescribed antibiotics and plenty of bed rest.*

intransitive **1.** To establish rules, laws, or directions. **2.** To order a medicine or other treatment.

[Middle English *prescriben,* from Latin *praescrībere* : *prae-,* pre- + *scrībere,* to write.]

RELATED WORD:

noun—**pre·scrib′er**

SEE NOTE AT **proscribe** (# 78).

75

pres·ent·ly (prĕz′ənt-lē)

adverb

1. In a short time; soon: *"She thought she must have been mistaken at first, for none of the scarecrows in Kansas ever wink; but presently the figure nodded its head to her in a friendly way"* (L. Frank Baum, *The Wonderful Wizard of Oz*). **2.** USAGE PROBLEM At this time or period; now: *Springfield is presently the capital of Illinois.*

The original use of *presently* to mean "at the present time, currently" goes back to the late 1300s. This usage seems to have disappeared from the written record in the 1600s, but it probably survived in speech, as it is widely found nowadays in both speech and writing. Perhaps because this sense was not treated in dictionaries until relatively recently, some language critics have argued that this usage is an error and that *presently* should only be used in the sense of "in a short time, soon," as in the shopkeeper's *I will be with you presently.* In four surveys from 1965 to 1999, only 47–50 percent of the Usage Panel accepted the "currently" usage in sentences like *She is presently the secretary of state.* By 2011, 63 percent found this sentence acceptable. So, although many still adhere to this guideline, resistance appears to be waning.

"While Dorothy was looking earnestly into the queer, painted face of the Scarecrow, she was surprised to see one of the eyes slowly wink at her. She thought she must have been mistaken at first, for none of the scarecrows in Kansas ever wink; but **presently** the figure nodded its head to her in a friendly way. Then she climbed down from the fence and walked up to it, while Toto ran around the pole and barked."

—L. Frank Baum,
The Wonderful Wizard of Oz

prin·ci·pal (prĭn′sə-pəl)

adjective

1. First, highest, or foremost in importance, rank, worth, or degree; chief: *The principal character in* Gone With the Wind *is Scarlett O'Hara.* **2.** Of, relating to, or being a financial principal, or a principal in a financial transaction.

noun

1. A person who holds a position of presiding rank, especially the head of an elementary school or high school: *The rowdy students were sent to the principal's office.* **2.** A main participant, as in a business deal. **3.** A person having a leading or starring role: *The director cast the chorus before casting the principals.* **4a.** A financial holding as distinguished from the interest or revenue from it. **b.** A sum of money owed as a debt, upon which interest is calculated.

[Middle English, from Old French, from Latin *prīncipālis*, from *prīnceps, prīncip-*, leader, emperor.]

RELATED WORDS:

adverb—**prin′ci·pal·ly**
noun—**prin′ci·pal·ship′**

Principal and *principle* are often confused but have no meanings in common. *Principle* is only a noun and usually refers to a rule or standard: *The class was assigned to read an essay about the principles of democracy. Principal* is both a noun and an adjective. As a noun, in general usage it refers to a person who holds a high position or plays an important role: *A meeting was held among all the principals in the transaction.* As an adjective it has the sense of "chief" or "leading": *The coach's principal concern is the quarterback's health.*

77

prin·ci·ple (prĭn′sə-pəl)

noun

1. A basic truth or statement, especially a system of beliefs or ideals: *The senator swore to uphold the principles of democracy.* **2a.** A rule or standard, especially of good behavior: *The sheriff was a man of principle.* **b.** The general set of moral or ethical standards: *"He chose principle over partisanship and is respected by liberals and conservatives alike"* (Brent Staples, *New York Times Book Review*). **3.** A statement or set of statements describing the functioning of natural phenomena or mechanical processes: *"Quantum teleportation makes use of a strange aspect of quantum physics called the Heisenberg Uncertainty Principle, which says it is impossible to measure both the speed and position of an object at the same time"* (Peter O'Connor, *Star Tribune* [Minneapolis]).

IDIOMS:

in principle With regard to the basics: *"Monitoring systems can in principle be programmed to look for certain keywords, like bomb or target, within messages they capture"* (Susan Stellin, *New York Times*).

on principle According to or because of principle: *Because I am an environmentalist, I objected to the airport's expansion into the marsh on principle.*

[Middle English, alteration of Old French *principe,* from Latin *prīncipium,* from *prīnceps, prīncip-*, leader, emperor.]

SEE NOTE AT **principal** (# 76).

78 **pro·scribe** (prō-skrīb′)

transitive verb

Past participle and past tense: **pro·scribed**
Present participle: **pro·scrib·ing**
Third person singular present tense: **pro·scribes**

1. To forbid; prohibit: *The government proscribes the importation of certain plants.* **2.** To denounce; condemn: *"In June 1580, Philip II had proscribed William as 'the chief disturber of our state of Christendom' and offered twenty-five thousand ecus to anyone who might venture to kill him"* (Simon Schama, *American Scholar*). **3.** To banish; outlaw: *After the coup, the monarch was proscribed and ordered to leave the country.*

[Middle English *proscriben,* from Latin *prōscrībere,* to put up someone's name as outlawed : *prō-,* in front + *scrībere,* to write.]

RELATED WORD:

noun—**pro·scrib′er**

Some senses of *prescribe* and *proscribe* are opposite in meaning. But because the two words sound similar, they're often confused. In its most common senses, *proscribe* means "to forbid" and "to denounce." *Prescribe,* on the other hand, means "to set down as a rule or guide," as in *The company handbook prescribes acceptable ways of reassigning an employee.* The medical sense, "to order the use of a medicine or treatment," as in *The doctor prescribed two aspirin,* is related to this sense.

79 **re·nown** (rĭ-noun′)

noun

The quality of being widely honored and acclaimed; fame.

[Middle English *renoun,* from Anglo-Norman, from *re-nomer,* to make famous : *re-*, repeatedly + *nomer,* to name (from Latin *nōmināre,* from *nōmen, nōmin-*, name).]

RELATED WORD:

adjective—**re·nowned′**

Because *renown* means "fame," and to be famous is to be well-known, *renown* is often misspelled with a *k.* For the same reasons, *renown* is often mispronounced as though it rhymed with *own. Renown* is properly pronounced with the same vowel sound as *noun* or *town.* The same holds true for the adjectival form, *renowned.*

80

ret·i·cent (rĕt′ĭ-sənt)

adjective

1. Inclined to keep one's thoughts, feelings, and personal affairs to oneself: *"The cowboy was usually soft-spoken and reserved of manner with strangers, so much so that he gained the reputation of being taciturn and reticent by nature, a conclusion which was erroneous"* (Ramon F. Adams, *Cowboy Lingo*). **2.** USAGE PROBLEM Reluctant; unwilling.

[Latin *reticēns, reticent-* present participle of *reticēre,* to keep silent : *re-,* re- + *tacēre,* to be silent.]

RELATED WORD:

adverb—**ret′i·cent·ly**

Reticent is generally used to indicate a reluctance to speak. Many people criticize its extended use as an all-purpose synonym for *reluctant.* In a 2001 survey, 83 percent of the Usage Panel found unacceptable the sentence *A lot of out-of-towners are reticent to come to the Twin Cities for a ballgame if there's a chance the game will be rained out.*

81 **sac·ri·le·gious** (săk′rə-lĭj′əs, săk′rə-lē′jəs)

adjective

Grossly irreverent toward what is or is held to be sacred: *"Most sacrilegious murder hath broke ope / The Lord's anointed temple"* (William Shakespeare, *Macbeth*).

[From *sacrilege* (from Old French, from Latin *sacrilegium*, from *sacrilegus*, one who steals sacred things : *sacer*, sacred + *legere*, to gather) + *-ous*, adjectival suffix.]

RELATED WORDS:

noun—**sac′ri·lege** (săk′rə-lĭj)
adverb—**sac′ri·le′gious·ly**
noun—**sac′ri·le′gious·ness**

✎ *Sacrilegious*, the adjective form of *sacrilege*, is often misspelled with the first *i* and the *e* switched, through confusion with the word *religious*.

82 **sea·son·a·ble** (sē′zə-nə-bəl)

adjective

1. In keeping with the time or the season: *"The weather was fair and seasonable, but Mary wore flannel underclothes beneath her dress and a heavy cloak as well"* (Michael Crummey, *River Thieves*). **2.** Occurring or performed at the proper time; timely: *The pundits praised the government's seasonable intervention in the trade dispute.*

RELATED WORD:

adverb—**sea′son·a·bly**

SEE NOTE AT **seasonal** (# 83).

83

sea·son·al (sē′zə-nəl)

adjective

Of or dependent on a particular season: "*Among the important soil properties are natural soil drainage, permeability, . . . load bearing capacity, depth to water table, seasonal wetness, shrink-swell capacity and soil structure*" (Bobbi McDermott, *Yuma Sun*).

RELATED WORD:

adverb—**sea′son·al·ly**

Seasonal and *seasonable*, though closely related, have different uses. *Seasonal* applies to what depends on or is controlled by the season of the year: *a seasonal increase in employment. Seasonable* applies to what is appropriate to the season (*seasonable clothing*) or timely (*seasonable intervention*). Rains are *seasonal* if they occur at a certain time of the year; they are *seasonable* at any time if they save the crops.

84 **sen·su·al** (sĕn′sho͞o-əl)

adjective

1. Of, relating to, given to, or providing gratification of the physical and especially the sexual appetites: *"The modern geisha is the aristocrat of the huge industry that has evolved through the centuries to cater to Japanese men's sensual desires"* (Jodi Cobb, *National Geographic*). **2.** Relating to or affecting any of the senses or a sense organ; sensory.

RELATED WORDS:

adverb—**sen′su·al·ly**
noun—**sen′su·al·ness**

SEE NOTE AT **sensuous** (# 85).

85

sen·su·ous (sĕn′sho͞o-əs)

adjective

1. Of, relating to, or derived from the senses: "*[T]hough he turned the pages with the sensuous joy of the book-lover, he did not know what he was reading, and one book after another dropped from his hand*" (Edith Wharton, *The Age of Innocence*). **2.** Appealing to or gratifying the senses: *The sculpture featured sensuous curves juxtaposed with sharp facial features.* **3.** Easily affected through the senses.

RELATED WORDS:

adverb—**sen′su·ous·ly**

noun—**sen′su·ous·ness**

Both *sensual* and *sensuous* mean "relating to or gratifying the senses." *Sensuous* can refer to any of the senses but usually applies to those involved in aesthetic enjoyment, as of art or music: *The critic lectured about the sensuous imagery in 19th century poems. Sensual* more often applies to the physical senses or appetites, particularly those associated with sexual pleasure.

"[T]hough he turned the pages with the **sensuous** joy of the book-lover, he did not know what he was reading, and one book after another dropped from his hand. Suddenly, among them, he lit on a small volume of verse which he had ordered because the name had attracted him: "The House of Life." He took it up, and found himself plunged in an atmosphere unlike any he had ever breathed in books; so warm, so rich, and yet so ineffably tender, that it gave a new and haunting beauty to the most elementary of human passions."

—Edith Wharton,
The Age of Innocence

set (sĕt)

verb

Past participle and past tense: **set**

Present participle: **set·ting**

Third person singular present tense: **sets**

transitive **1.** To put in a specified position; place: *I set the book on the shelf.* **2.** To put into a specified state: *With a push he set the wagon in motion.* **3.** To put into a stable position: *She set the fence post into a bed of concrete.* **4.** To restore to a proper and normal state when dislocated or broken: *The doctor set the broken bone.* **5.** To adjust for proper functioning: *We set the mouse traps to prevent infestation.* **6.** To adjust (an instrument, tool, or device) so that some desired condition of operation is established: *She set the alarm clock for 7:00.* **7.** To arrange tableware on or at in preparation for a meal: "*'Where's Papa going with that ax?' said Fern to her mother as they were setting the table for breakfast*" (E.B. White, *Charlotte's Web*). **8.** To arrange (hair) in a certain style, as by rolling it up with clips and curlers. **9a.** To arrange (type) into words and sentences in preparation for printing. **b.** To arrange (matter to be printed) into type. **10a.** To compose (music) to fit a given text. **b.** To write (words) to fit a melody. **11.** To represent the unfolding of (a drama or narrative, for instance) in a specific place: *The play* Romeo and Juliet *is set in Verona.* **12.** To make as a rule or guideline; establish: *You should set an example for your younger brother.* **13.** To decide on; appoint or designate: *They set June 6 as the day of the wedding.* **14.** To detail or assign (someone) to a particular duty, service, or station: *The guards were set around the perimeter.* **15a.** To put in a mounting; mount: *The jeweler set an emerald in a pendant.* **b.** To apply jewels to; stud: *The museum displayed a tiara that was set with diamonds.* **16.** To cause to sit:

The host set the woozy guest on the couch. **17.** To position (oneself) in such a way as to be ready to start running a race. **18.** To pass (a volleyball), usually with the fingertips, in an arc close to the net so that a teammate can drive it over the net. **19.** To fix at a given amount: *The judge set bail for the defendant at $50,000.* **20.** To point to the location of (game) by holding a fixed attitude. Used of a hunting dog.

intransitive **1.** To disappear below the horizon: *The sun set at seven that evening.* **2.** To sit on eggs. Used of fowl: *The hens were setting.* **3.** To become fixed; harden: *It will take 12 hours for the cement to set.* **4.** To become permanent. Used of dye. **5.** To become whole; knit. Used of a broken bone. **6.** NONSTANDARD To sit.

[Middle English *setten,* from Old English *settan.*]

The verbs *set* and *sit* have been confused since the Middle Ages, so it is not surprising that they sometimes get mixed up today. Throughout its history *set* has been a transitive verb. It originally meant "to cause (someone) to sit" and also "to cause (something) to be in a certain position." This second sense survives as a basic meaning of the verb today: *She set the book on the table.* But since about 1300, *set* has been used without an object to mean "to be in a seated position, sit." *Set* is still common as a nonstandard or regional word meaning "sit," especially in rural speech: *Stop on by and set a spell.* The most familiar of *set*'s intransitive uses describes the motion of the sun at the end of the day. The sun only *sets;* it never *sits.*

This would seem a bit anomalous, since *sit* is mainly an intransitive verb. Its basic meaning is "to rest supported on the hindquarters," as in *He sits at the table.* It has a variety of other uses that entail occupying a location (*The house sits on a small lot*) or existing in a resting or unused state (*The skis sat gathering dust*). Nevertheless, *sit* has its transitive uses, some of which date back to the 14th century. It has taken over the meaning that originally belonged to *set,* "to cause (someone) to sit," so that we can now say *They sat the winning ticket holder back in his chair.* A more recent transitive use of *sit* is "to provide seats for," as in *The theater sits 2,000.*

Fortunately, you don't have to worry about chickens. A hen can *sit* or *set* on her eggs, so in this usage you can't go wrong.

sex (sĕks)

noun

1a. The property or quality by which organisms are classified as female or male on the basis of their reproductive organs and functions: *Through amniocentesis, the sex of a developing fetus can be determined.* **b.** Either of the two divisions, designated female and male, of this classification: *The college's policy is that no student is allowed to have visitors of the opposite sex after midnight.* **2.** Females or males considered as a group. **3.** The condition or character of being female or male; the physiological, functional, and psychological differences that distinguish the female and the male. **4.** Sexual intercourse.

[Middle English, from Latin *sexus*.]

SEE NOTE AT **gender** (# 40).

sit (sĭt)

verb

Past participle and past tense: **sat**
Present participle: **sit·ting**
Third person singular present tense: **sits**

intransitive **1a.** To rest with the torso vertical and the body supported on the buttocks: *"I was leaning against a bar in a speakeasy on Fifty-second Street, waiting for Nora to finish her Christmas shopping, when a girl got up from the table where she had been sitting with three other people and came over to me"* (Dashiell Hammett, *The Thin Man*). **b.** To rest with the hindquarters lowered onto a supporting surface. Used of animals: *The dog sat at the foot of my bed.* **c.** To perch. Used of birds. **d.** To cover eggs for hatching; brood: *The hen sat on her eggs.* **2.** To be situated or located: *The farmhouse sits on a hill.* **3.** To lie or rest: *The dishes are sitting on a shelf.* **4.** To pose for an artist or photographer. **5.** To occupy a seat as a member of a body of officials: *Gerald Ford sat in Congress before becoming president.* **6.** To be in session: *The Supreme Court does not normally sit in the summer.* **7.** To remain inactive or unused: *Your expensive skis are sitting gathering dust in the corner.* **8.** To affect one with or as if with a burden; weigh: *Official duties sat heavily upon the governor's mind.* **9.** To fit, fall, or drape in a specified manner: *That jacket sits perfectly on you.* **10.** To be agreeable to one; please: *The idea didn't sit well with any of us.* **11.** To keep watch or take care of a child; babysit: *On weekends, I make extra money by sitting for the neighbors.*

intransitive **1.** To cause to sit; seat: *The ushers sat the wedding guests in the pews.* **2.** To sit on (eggs) for the purpose of hatching. **3.** To provide seating accommodation for: *This concert hall sits 1,000 people.*

[Middle English *sitten,* from Old English *sittan.*]

SEE NOTE AT **set** (# 86).

that (thăt, thət)

pronoun

Plural **those** (*th*ōz)

1. Used to refer to the one designated, implied, mentioned, or understood: *What kind of soup is that?* **2.** Used to indicate the farther or less immediate one: *That is for sale; this is not.* **3. those** Used to indicate an unspecified number of people: *The aide wrote down the names of those who refused to attend the meeting.* **4.** Used as a relative pronoun to introduce a clause, especially a restrictive clause: *They towed the car that had the flat tire.* **5.** In, on, by, or with which: *The director returns to New York City each summer that the concerts are performed.*

adjective

Plural **those** *(thōz)*

1. Being the one singled out, implied, or understood: *Those mountains are seventy miles away.* **2.** Being the one further removed or less obvious: *That route is shorter than this one.*

adverb

1. To such an extent or degree: *Is your problem that complicated?* **2.** To a high degree; very: *No one took what he said that seriously.*

conjunction

1. Used to introduce a subordinate clause stating a result, wish, purpose, reason, or cause: *She hoped that he would arrive on time. He was saddened that she felt so little for him.* **2a.** Used to introduce an anticipated subordinate clause following the expletive *it* occurring as subject of the verb: *It is true that dental work is expensive.* **b.** Used to introduce a subordinate clause modifying an adverb or adverbial expression: *They will go anywhere that they are welcome.* **c.** Used to introduce a subordinate clause that is joined to an adjective or noun as a complement: *She was sure that she was right. It is his belief that rates will rise soon.* **3.** Used to introduce a noun clause that is usually the subject or object of a verb or a predicate nominative: *"That America is richer today* [as compared to 100 years ago] *almost goes without saying"* (Peter Grier, *Christian Science Monitor*).

IDIOM

that is To explain more clearly; in other words: *The bakery is on the first floor, that is, the floor at street level.*

[Middle English, from Old English *thæt.*]

✎ The standard rule requires that *that* should be used only to introduce a restrictive (or defining) relative clause, which identifies the entity being talked about; in this use it should never be preceded by a comma. Thus, in the sentence *The house that Jack built has been torn down,* the clause *that Jack built* is a restrictive clause identifying the specific house that was torn down. Similarly, in *I am looking for a book that is easy to read,* the restrictive clause *that is easy to read* tells what kind of book is desired. A related rule stipulates that *which* should be used with nonrestrictive (or nondefining) clauses, which give additional information about an entity that has already been identified in the context; in this use, *which* is always preceded by a comma. Thus, we say *The students in Chemistry 101 have been complaining about the textbook, which* (not *that*) *is hard to follow.* The clause *which is hard to follow* is nonrestrictive in that it does not indicate which text is being complained about; even if the clause were omitted, we would know that the phrase *the textbook* refers to the text in Chemistry 101.

Some grammarians extend the rule and insist that, just as *that* should be used only in restrictive clauses, *which* should be used only in nonrestrictive clauses. Thus, they suggest that we should avoid sentences such as *I need a book which will tell me all about city gardening,* where the restrictive clause *which will tell me all about city gardening* indicates which sort of book is needed. But this extension of the rule is far from universally accepted, and the use of *which* with restrictive clauses is common. Furthermore, since *that* cannot be used with clauses introduced by a preposition (whether or not restrictive), *which* is used with both clauses when such a clause is joined by *and* or *or* to another that does not begin with a preposition, as in *It is a philosophy in which the common man may find solace and which many have found reason to praise.* Such constructions are often considered cumbersome, however, and it may be best to recast the sentence completely to avoid the problem.

That is often omitted in a relative clause when the subject of the clause is different from the word that the clause refers to. Thus, we may say either *the book that I was reading* or *the book I was reading.* In addition, *that* is commonly omitted before other kinds of subordinate clauses, as in *I think we should try again* where *that* would precede *we.* These constructions omitting *that* are entirely idiomatic, even in more formal contexts.

90

un·ex·cep·tion·a·ble (ŭn′ĭk-sĕp′shə-nə-bəl)

adjective

Beyond any reasonable objection; irreproachable: *Our accounting firm holds itself to the highest standards; therefore, any of its findings I believe to be unexceptionable.*

RELATED WORD:

adverb—**un′ex·cep′tion·a·bly**

The confusion between *unexceptionable* and *unexceptional* is understandable, since both derive from the noun *exception. Unexceptionable* takes its meaning from *exception* in the sense "objection," as in the idiom *take exception to* ("find fault with, object to"). Thus *unexceptionable* is commendatory, meaning "not open to any objection or criticism," as in *A judge's ethical standards should be unexceptionable. Unexceptional,* by contrast, is related to the adjective *exceptional* ("outstanding, above average"), which takes its meaning from *exception* in the sense "an unusual case"; thus *unexceptional* generally has a somewhat negative meaning, "not superior, run-of-the-mill" as in *Some judges' ethical standards, sadly, have been unexceptional.*

91 **un·ex·cep·tion·al** (ŭn′ĭk-sĕp′shə-nəl)

adjective

Not varying from a norm; usual: *The professor gave the unexceptional paper a C.*

RELATED WORD:

adverb—**un′ex·cep′tion·al·ly**

SEE NOTE AT **unexceptionable** (# 90).

92 un·in·ter·est·ed (ŭn-ĭn′trĭ-stĭd, ŭn-ĭn′tər-ĭ-stĭd, ŭn-ĭn′tə-rĕs′tĭd)

adjective

1. Marked by or exhibiting a lack of interest: *Uninterested voters led to a low turnout on Election Day.* **2.** Having no stake or interest; impartial: *Both sides requested a mediator who was uninterested in the dispute.*

RELATED WORDS:

adverb—**un·in′ter·est·ed·ly**
noun—**un·in′ter·est·ed·ness**

SEE NOTE AT **disinterested** (# 27).

93 u·nique (yo͞o-nēk′)

adjective

1. Being the only one of its kind: *The scholar studied the unique existing example of the eighteenth-century author's handwriting.* **2.** Without an equal or equivalent; unparalleled: *The one-time offer presented them with a unique opportunity to buy a house.* **3.** Characteristic of a particular category, condition, or locality: *The marine biologist examined weather patterns unique to coastal areas.*

[French, from Old French, from Latin *ūnicus.*]

RELATED WORDS:

adverb—**u·nique′ly**
noun—**u·nique′ness**

Unique may be the foremost example of an absolute term—a term that, in the eyes of traditional grammarians, should not allow comparison or modification by an adverb of degree like *very, somewhat,* or *quite.* Thus, most grammarians believe that it is incorrect to say that something is *very unique* or *more unique than* something else, though phrases such as *nearly unique* and *almost unique* are presumably acceptable, since in these cases *unique* is not modified by an adverb of degree. A substantial majority of the Usage Panel supports the traditional view. In our 2004 survey, 66 percent of the Panelists disapproved of the sentence *Her designs are quite unique in today's fashion,* although in our 1988 survey, 80 percent rejected this same sentence, suggesting that resistance to this usage may be waning.

In fact, the nontraditional modification of *unique* may be found in the work of many reputable writers and has certainly been put to effective use: "*I am in the rather unique position of being the son, the grandson, and the great-grandson of preachers*" (Martin Luther King, Jr.). "*The creature is so unique in its style and appearance that the biologists who discovered it have given it not just its own species name... but have moved way up the classification scale and declared that it is an entirely new phylum*" (Natalie Angier).

u·til·ize (yo͞ot′l-īz′)

transitive verb

Past participle and past tense: **u·til·ized**
Present participle: **u·til·iz·ing**
Third person singular present tense: **u·til·iz·es**

To put to use, especially for a practical purpose: "*The . . . group has genetically engineered the bacterium so that more glucose is diverted toward the other main chemical pathway within the organism that utilizes the sugar*" (Gary Stix, *Scientific American*).

[French *utiliser,* from Italian *utilizzare,* from *utile,* useful, from Latin *ūtilis,* from *ūtī,* to use.]

RELATED WORDS:

noun—**u′til·i·za′tion**
noun—**u′til·iz′er**

A number of critics have remarked that *utilize* is an unnecessary substitute for *use.* It is true that many occurrences of *utilize* could be replaced by *use* with no loss to anything but pretentiousness, for example, in sentences such as *They utilized questionable methods in their analysis* or *We hope that many commuters will continue to utilize mass transit after the bridge has reopened.* But *utilize* can mean "to find a profitable or practical use for." Thus the sentence *The teachers were unable to use the new computers* might mean only that the teachers were unable to operate the computers, whereas *The teachers were unable to utilize the new computers* suggests that the teachers could not find ways to employ the computers in instruction.

95 **weight** (wāt)

noun

1. A measure of the heaviness of an object: *The weight of the car is 3,000 pounds.* **2.** The force with which a body is attracted to Earth or another celestial body, equal to the product of the object's mass and the acceleration of gravity. **3a.** A unit measure of gravitational force: *Comprehensive reference works contain a table of weights and measures.* **b.** A system of such measures: *Gemstones are measured using a system of measurement called "troy weight."* **4.** An object used principally to exert a force by virtue of its gravitational attraction to Earth, such as a paperweight or a dumbbell. **5.** A load or burden; oppressiveness: *"Adding features to run complex software adds weight and bogs down portability"* (Eric C. Evarts, *Christian Science Monitor).* **6.** Influence, importance, or authority: *Her opinion carries great weight in the medical community.*

transitive verb

Past participle and past tense: **weight·ed**
Present participle: **weight·ing**
Third person singular present tense: **weights**

1. To make heavy or heavier with a weight or weights: *"Marine mud [is] a blue-gray mud that settled 15,000 years ago while much of Maine was weighted down with glacial ice and Boston was underwater"* (Jamie Kageleiry & Christine Schultz, *Yankee Magazine*). **2.** To load down, burden, or oppress: *Until an extra associate was hired, I was weighted with heavy responsibilities at work.*

[Middle English *wight,* from Old English *wiht.*]

SEE NOTE AT **mass** (# 61).

96

where·fore (hwâr′fôr′, wâr′fôr′)

adverb

For what purpose or reason; why: *"O Romeo, Romeo! wherefore art thou Romeo?"* (William Shakespeare, *Romeo and Juliet*).

noun

A purpose or cause: *The editorial explained all the whys and wherefores of the tax proposal.*

Many people mistakenly assume that *wherefore* is a synonym of *where* based on a misreading of one of Shakespeare's most well-known lines. Many mistakenly interpret Juliet's balcony speech as questioning Romeo's location (who as it turns out happens to be just below the balcony). However, Juliet is not asking *where* Romeo is. She is asking *why* Romeo is Romeo—that is, she wants to know why her love is who he is: a member of the family with whom her family has been feuding.

"O Romeo, Romeo! **wherefore** art thou Romeo?
Deny thy father and refuse thy name;
Or, if thou wilt not, be but sworn my love,
And I'll no longer be a Capulet."

—William Shakespeare,
Romeo and Juliet

which (hwĭch, wĭch)

pronoun

1. What particular one or ones: *Which of these books is yours?* **2.** The one or ones previously mentioned or implied, specifically: **a.** Used as a relative pronoun in a clause that provides additional information about the antecedent: *I want to renovate my house, which is small and old.* **b.** Used as a relative pronoun preceded by *that* or a preposition in a clause that defines or restricts the antecedent: *The clerk provided him with that which he requested. I was fascinated by the subject on which she spoke.* **c.** Used instead of *that* as a relative pronoun in a clause that defines or restricts the antecedent: *The movie which was shown later was better.* **3.** Any of the things, events, or people designated or implied; whichever: *Choose which you like best.* **4.** A thing or circumstance that: *They left early, which was wise.*

adjective

1. What particular one or ones of a number of things or people: *Which part of town do you mean?* **2.** Any one or any number of; whichever: *Use which door you please.* **3.** Being the one or ones previously mentioned or implied: *It started to rain, at which point we ran.*

[Middle English, from Old English *hwilc.*]

✍ The relative pronoun *which* is sometimes used to refer to an entire sentence or clause, rather than a noun or noun phrase, as in *They ignored me, which proved to be unwise. They swept the council elections, which could never have happened under the old rules.* While these examples are unexceptionable, using *which* in this way sometimes produces an ambiguous sentence. Thus *It emerged that Chris made the complaint, which surprised everybody* leaves unclear whether it was surprising that a complaint was made or that Chris made it. The ambiguity can be avoided with paraphrases such as *It emerged that the complaint was made by Chris, a revelation that surprised everybody.*

ALSO SEE NOTE AT **that** (# 89).

98 **wreak** (rēk)

transitive verb

Past participle and past tense: **wreaked**
Present participle: **wreak·ing**
Third person singular present tense: **wreaks**

1. To inflict (vengeance or punishment) upon a person: *"I at last devised a desperate plan that would not only blow my wedding to pieces but would wreak a terrible revenge on my parents and my betrothed"* (Louis Auchincloss, *DeCicco v. Schweizer*). **2.** To express or gratify (anger, malevolence, or resentment); vent: *"In his little evil brain he sought for some excuse to wreak his hatred upon Tarzan"* (Edgar Rice Burroughs, *Tarzan of the Apes*). **3.** To bring about; cause: *"A harmful recessive gene doesn't wreak havoc unless it exists in two copies"* (Jennifer Ackerman, *Chance in the House of Fate*).

[Middle English *wreken,* from Old English *wrecan.*]

Wreak is sometimes confused with *wreck,* perhaps because the wreaking of damage may leave a wreck: *The storm wreaked* (not *wrecked*) *havoc along the coast.* The past tense and past participle of *wreak* is *wreaked,* not *wrought,* which is an alternative past tense and past participle of *work.*

"In the morning, looking towards the sea side, the tide being low, I saw something lie on the shore bigger than ordinary, and it looked like a cask; when I came to it, I found a small barrel, and two or three pieces of the **wreck** of the ship, which were driven on shore by the late hurricane; and looking towards the **wreck** itself, I thought it seemed to lie higher out of the water than it used to do."

—Daniel Defoe,
Robinson Crusoe

99

wreck (rĕk)

noun

1. Accidental destruction of a ship; a shipwreck: *The wreck of the Titanic occurred in the Atlantic Ocean in April of 1912.* **2a.** The stranded hulk of a severely damaged ship: *"I found a small barrel, and two or three pieces of the wreck of the ship, which were driven on shore by the late hurricane"* (Daniel Defoe, *Robinson Crusoe*). **b.** Fragments of a ship or its cargo cast ashore by the sea after a shipwreck; wreckage. **3.** The remains of something that has been wrecked or ruined: *"Up went the axe again . . . four times the blow fell; . . . it was not until the fifth, that the lock burst and the wreck of the door fell inwards on the carpet"* (Robert Louis Stevenson, *The Strange Case of Dr. Jekyll and Mr. Hyde*). **4.** A person who is physically or mentally broken down or worn out.

verb

Past participle and past tense: **wrecked**
Present participle: **wreck·ing**
Third person singular present tense: **wrecks**

transitive **1.** To cause the destruction of (something) in or as if in a collision: *"The morning after the storm that has wrecked the ship and drowned his companions, Crusoe wakes on shore with only a pocket knife, a pipe, and a tin of tobacco"* (Hilary Masters, *Making It Up*). **2.** To dismantle or raze; tear down: *The contractor wrecked the old building to make way for the new apartment complex.* **3.** To cause to undergo ruin or disaster: *"I will not go along with a huge tax cut for the wealthy at the expense of everyone else and wreck our good economy in the process"* (Al Gore, speech to the Democratic National Convention).

intransitive To suffer destruction or ruin; become wrecked: *The ship wrecked in the shoals off the shore.*

[Middle English *wrek,* from Anglo-Norman *wrec,* of Scandinavian origin; akin to Old Norse *rec,* wreckage.]

SEE NOTE AT **wreak** (# 98).

100

zo·ol·o·gy (zō-ŏl′ə-jē, zo͞o-ŏl′ə-jē)

noun

1. The branch of biology that deals with animals and animal life, including the study of the structure, physiology, development, and classification of animals. **2.** The animal life of a particular area or period: *The professor lectured on the zoology of the Pleistocene.* **3.** The characteristics of a particular animal group or category: *In biology class, we had a unit on the zoology of mammals.*

RELATED WORD:

noun—**zo·ol′o·gist**

Traditionally, the first syllable of *zoology* has been pronounced as (zō), rhyming with *toe.* However, most likely due to the familiarity of the word *zoo* (which is merely a shortened form of *zoological garden*), the pronunciation of the first syllable as (zo͞o) is also commonly heard. In 1999, 88 percent of the Usage Panel found the (zō) pronunciation acceptable, and 60 percent found the (zo͞o) pronunciation acceptable. In their own speech, 68 percent of the Panelists use the (zō) pronunciation, and 32 percent use the (zo͞o) pronunciation. Thus, while both pronunciations can be considered acceptable, the (zō) pronunciation may be perceived as more scientific.